THE COMPLETE BOOK OF
DOGS

THE COMPLETE BOOK OF
DOGS

A. J. AND H. A. BARKER

LONGMEADOW
P R E S S

This 1992 edition published by
Longmeadow Press
201 High Ridge Road
Stamford CT 06904

Produced by
Brompton Books Corporation
15 Sherwood Place
Greenwich CT 06830

ISBN 0-681-41766-8

Printed in Hong Kong

0 9 8 7 6 5 4 3 2

Captions, front jacket: Bernese Mountain Dogs.
Back jacket: Golden Retriever with puppy.
Jacket flaps: The authors with their Cavalier King
Charles Spaniels.
Page 1: Samoyed.
Page 2/3: Beagle puppy.
Page 4/5: Bernese Mountain Dog with puppies.

CONTENTS

INTRODUCTION

The first dogs

For centuries, dogs have been part of the everyday life of people all over the world. Beloved by some, tolerated by others, and occasionally disliked, the dog is universally recognized as one of the most intelligent animals. Just how man and the creature which has been called his 'best friend' came to accept each other is a mystery. Originally they were enemies – rival hunters competing for similar foods – and up to the Stone Age period any kind of partnership between man and dog seems improbable. At that time the early dogs were akin to wolves, and prehistoric men and wolf-dogs were just as ready to eat each other as any other form of prey.

The domestication process took a long time, and we shall never know why or how it evolved. Perhaps the wolf-dogs prowled round man's encampments looking for opportunities to steal food or pick up a wandering child. Perhaps they were attracted by the bones and offal that men threw out of their caves, and these scraps forged a link between human and animal. In the course of the development of this relationship undoubtedly many dogs were killed. The first dogs were vicious brutes, but primitive men were equally vicious – wild creatures ready to defend their settlements against marauders with the same savagery they used in hunting. Nevertheless they had the rudimentary traits attributed to humans and, when dogs and orphaned puppies were caught, it was inevitable that some of them would be taken into the settlements. Having been reared by man, some of the puppies formed attachments with the people that fed them. Such dogs then began to identify themselves as members of the human family and their innate 'territorial' instinct led them to defend the territory of the humans that had adopted them against invaders – even their own species. With every succeeding generation of puppies born in the human settlements, the bond between man and dog grew stronger but the dogs retained their basic instincts. Primitive men feared darkness, for beyond the circle of light cast by the camp fire real and imaginary danger lurked wild animals and evil spirits, the latter no less worrying because of their immunity to attack. When it was realized that the settlement dogs were able to detect the approach of enemies long before human sentries noticed anything, they were put to work as guard dogs; through their highly developed sense of smell and hearing dogs could sense danger and raise the alarm. This enabled the men to prepare

Previous page, left: A Bearded Collie. This type of Collie was originally bred in Scotland strictly as a working dog, but in this century it is reared as a pet. Previous page, right: Ruby Cavalier King Charles Spaniel. The Cavalier breed originated in England where it was crossed with other spaniels as well as certain toy breeds from China and Japan.

Left: A working pack of Basset Hounds is on a training exercise. Bassets have long noses with well-opened nostrils, and are therefore very good at tracking.

themselves for an attack. It was a short step from guarding man to guarding his other animals. As man acquired domestic animals the dog was called upon to protect them and to keep them together, that is, to act as a shepherd, and in the course of time the dog has been increasingly used in this role in the service of society.

The second basic instinct retained by the dogs born and bred in man's settlements was that of hunting. They no longer had to hunt for food, of course, since man provided that, but the natural instinct to chase and kill remained. Consequently, when early man found out that his dogs would cooperate in the hunt, they were employed in this role also and were used either to drive game in the direction of an ambush or to drag it down. Hunting in this manner went on for hundreds of years while succeeding generations of both men and dogs steadily became more and more domesticated and more familiar with each other's ways.

Undoubtedly the dog has changed considerably since the Stone Age days of the wolf-dog, and some people find it difficult to understand how so many different shapes and sizes have descended from one common ancestor. The answer is that, before today's multitude of breeds came to be recognized, a process of natural evolu-

Above left : A Collie gathering sheep. Above : A Curly-coated Retriever makes an excellent gundog.

tion in different parts of the world created dogs suitable for their own particular environment and conditions. This process, divergence in type, took millions of years, with mutations happening all the time. An animal which was born differing from the norm would find that this either helped or hindered him in his daily life. If the divergence was helpful, then those with the same abnormality would tend to thrive and breed in greater numbers, while those who found their mutation was a handicap would usually succumb in the struggle for survival and disappear. Thus the abnormal would become the normal until, in turn, the species took another step up on the ladder of evolution. The modern breeds of sight hound provide an excellent example of the evolution process. The original wolf-dog is believed to have been a comparatively slow animal, relying first and foremost on its sensitive nose and acute sense of hearing to find its prey, and then on its perseverence and stamina to track and eventually to catch it. On the plains and in desert country, however, speed was all important, for that was the only means of escape open to wild game pursued by its enemies. In such circumstances speed and sight were more important in the dog than the ability to detect by nose and ear. Thus a new type evolved – a rangy, long-legged, swift hunter from which are descended all the modern coursing dogs, such as the Borzoi, Greyhound, Saluki, Whippet, and Irish Wolfhound.

Primitive man would not, of course, have had any knowledge of the breeding processes inherent in the evolution of the dog. However, as the centuries rolled by, hunters and farmers would recognize that like bred like, and that a courageous dog mated to a brave bitch would usually produce puppies of a similar temperament. This would not always occur, owing to the

interplay of genetical factors not understood at the time, but it was a good enough rule to ensure that breeders who required certain attributes in their dogs would stand a fair chance of success.

Thus, by trial and error, a variety of dogs were produced – large dogs and small dogs, dogs with straight legs and dogs with crooked legs, dogs with thin coats and dogs with profuse coats – in effect, all the types of dogs which we have today.

Finally, with the passage of time, as knowledge grew, breeding became more scientific and dogs were bred for specific purposes – guard dogs, sheepdogs, hounds, pet dogs, handsome dogs, and grotesque dogs – in fact, every kind of dog for work, sport, or amusement.

Far left: A Greyhound puppy. A strong, muscular dog, the Greyhound is capable of reaching speeds of up to 30mph over a short distance.
Left: The Smooth-coated and Long-coated Chihuahuas are the smallest breeds of dog in the world.
Below: These three Standard Poodles are beautifully groomed for a show. The two dogs on the left are trimmed in the lion, or Continental, clip and the one on the right in the Dutch, or puppy. clip.

Dogs in the classics and in legend

The Greeks and Romans loved dogs and writers and teachers of both nations wrote freely in praise of them. In Greek mythology, for example, Actaeon, a huntsman, surprised the moon goddess Diana while bathing, was changed by her into a stag and torn to pieces by his own hounds.

Geryon, another character in Greek mythology, was reputed to be a monster with three heads, whose oxen ate human flesh and were guarded by Orthos, a two-headed dog. In another Greek legend, Icarius, the King of Attica, was killed by men who had drunk his wine and concluded it was poisoned. Icarius' body was buried under a tree, and his daughter Erigone was directed to the spot by the howls of his dog Maera (the glistener). Erigone promptly hanged herself from the nearest tree and Icarius, Erigone, and the faithful Maera were all carried off to the heavens and changed into constellations – becoming the Wagoner, the Virgo, and the Canis Minor.

Another of the constellations is Orion, who in mythology was a giant hunter slain by Diana and who now roams the skies attended by his dogs Arctophomus (bear killer) and Ptoophagus (the glutton of Ptoon).

The Roman Emperor Hadrian is said to have ordered a State funeral for a dog as a reward for its lifetime of fidelity. This is a virtue for which dogs have been praised since ancient times, and one of the most famous examples is that of Argus, Ulysses' dog. This dog had been parted from his master for over 20 years and was very old when Ulysses, disguised as a beggar, returned to his palace in Troy. An old servant who had known Ulysses since childhood failed to recognize him but in the words of the *Odyssey:*

> Near to the gates . . .
> Argus the dog his ancient master
>   knew,
> And, not unconscious of the voice
>   and tread,
> Lifts to the sound his ears, and rears
>   his head,
> He knew his Lord, he knew, and
>   strove to meet;
> In vain he strove to crawl and kiss
>   his feet:
> Yet all he could, his tail, his ears, his
>   eyes
> Salute his Master and confess his
>   joys.

Dragon, a dog owned by a certain Aubry of Montdidier, earned his place in legend for a different reason. In 1371 Aubry was murdered in the forest of Bondy near Paris. Nobody saw the murder, but suspicion fell on Richard of Macaire because a snarling Dragon flew at his throat. Richard, who was ordered by the judicial authorities to fight it out with the dog, was killed, and just before he died he confessed to the crime.

King Arthur is perhaps the best-known character in British mythology and his favorite hound was Cavall. Sir Tristam, one of the knights of Arthur's Round Table, whose exploits are recorded in Malory's *Morte d'Arthur,* is said to have had a dog called Hodain or Leon.

In Celtic mythology the foremost hero-figure was a mortal endowed with super-human faculties, Cú Chulainn. His name, which meant 'Hound of Chulann,' was given to him when he was seven years old after he had been compelled to kill the guard dog of Chulann the smith. But Cú Chulainn loved dogs and his favorite was called Luath – a name which Robert Burns subsequently gave to his own favorite dog and to the poor man's dog representing the peasantry in his poem *The Twa Dogs:*

> A ploughman's collie,
> A rhyming, ranting, raving billie
> Wha for his friend and comrade had
>   him,
> And in his freaks had Luath ca'd
>   him
> After some dog in Highland sang
> Was made lang syne – Lord knows
>   how lang.

Fingal, the great Gaelic semimythological hero, whose name was given to the great cavern on Staffa which is supposed to have been his home, had a dog called Bran. And the favorite of Roderick, a Spanish hero around whom many legends have been collected, was called Theron.

Then there is the legend of the Mauthe dog – a ghostly black spaniel which for many years haunted Peel Castle on the Isle of Man. It was said to go into the guardroom at dusk and, while this specter dog was there, the soldiers dare not swear or mouth obscenities. This was because a drunken trooper had on one occasion uttered a string of oaths, lost his speech and died three days later. (Sir Walter Scott refers to this dog in his *Lay of the Last Minstrel.)*

Beth Gelert, or the Grave of a Greyhound, is a ballad by William Robert Spencer, recounting an old and widespread legend

which, with variations, is found in Sanskrit and other ancient literature. Briefly, the story is that a Celtic chief Llewellyn, returning home from a day's hunting, is met by his favorite hound who is covered with blood. Llewellyn runs to see if anything has happened to his baby son, finds the cradle overturned and spattered with blood. Assuming the dog had attacked the child and eaten it, Llewellyn promptly stabs the hound to death. Afterward he finds the baby quite safe, and a huge wolf under the bed, dead.

Finally there is the tale of the *Dog of the Seven Sleepers*, Katmir, who, according to Moslem tradition, was admitted to heaven. (This was a special privilege, because dogs are generally disliked by Hindus and Moslems. One exception is made with the latter; the Arabs do not like dogs except for the Saluki, which is allowed to live in the tents and is bred with great care. An Arab cannot do any man a greater honor than by presenting him with the gift of a Saluki.)

This Eskimo Dog, photographed on the Eiger Glacier, Switzerland, is used for pulling sleds and for rescuing victims of avalanches. The St Bernard has also been used for rescue work, but the Eskimo Dog is swifter and more efficient.

ANATOMY OF THE DOG

It will be appreciated that body shape necessarily varies according to the type of dog, but the skeletons of all breeds contain – with a few minor exceptions – the same number of separate bones. There are, for example, seven cervical (neck) vertebrae and 13 thoracic vertebrae, each carrying a pair of ribs (see below). However, the relative sizes and relationship of the bones will vary according to the type of dog. Thus, in a tall breed such as the Irish Wolfhound, the bones will nearly all be long, while in a short, compact breed like the Pug they will nearly all be short. In between these extremes is a multitude of other breeds in which some bones are long and some short. A Whippet has long cervical and thoracic vertebrae and long legs; a Dachshund has long thoracic but short cervical vertebrae and very short legs. A Bull Terrier has a long neck and a short back, while a Staffordshire Bull Terrier is short in both places. Some breeds, such as the Old English Sheepdog, Dobermann, Pembroke Corgi, Schipperke, and Miniature Pinscher, have little or no tail and the number of tail bones is consequently less than in breeds having long tails.

The dog's head is the one feature which imparts individuality to the breed and there are some remarkable variations in the skull. To describe these variations, canine terms are used. Thus a Greyhound is said to have a 'lean' head, meaning one with a tight skin and without much flesh, the Chihuahua's rounded skull is said to be 'domed,' and the Pointer 'dish-faced.' Pendulous upper lips are 'flews' and loose, pendulous skin under the chin – a characteristic of the Bloodhound – is the 'dewlap.'

Above: Pembroke Welsh Corgis playing. The Pembroke Corgi is slightly lower set and smaller than the Cardigan, and its tail is docked.

Right: Muscular anatomy. Below right: Exterior anatomy. Below: Skeletal anatomy.

Occiput
Eye socket or orbit
Atlas
Axis
Cervical vertebrae
Thoracic vertebrae
Lumbar vertebrae
Pelvi
Shoulder blade or scapula
Femu
Humerus
Ribs
Ulna
Tibia
Radius
Fibula
Tarsu or hoc
Carpus
Metatarsu
Metacarpus or pastern

Previous page, left: The Weimaraner has an excellent nose and is useful for both tracking and retrieving. Previous page, right: The red and white colouring of this Irish setter is extremely rare. Most Irish Setters have a rich chestnut coat.

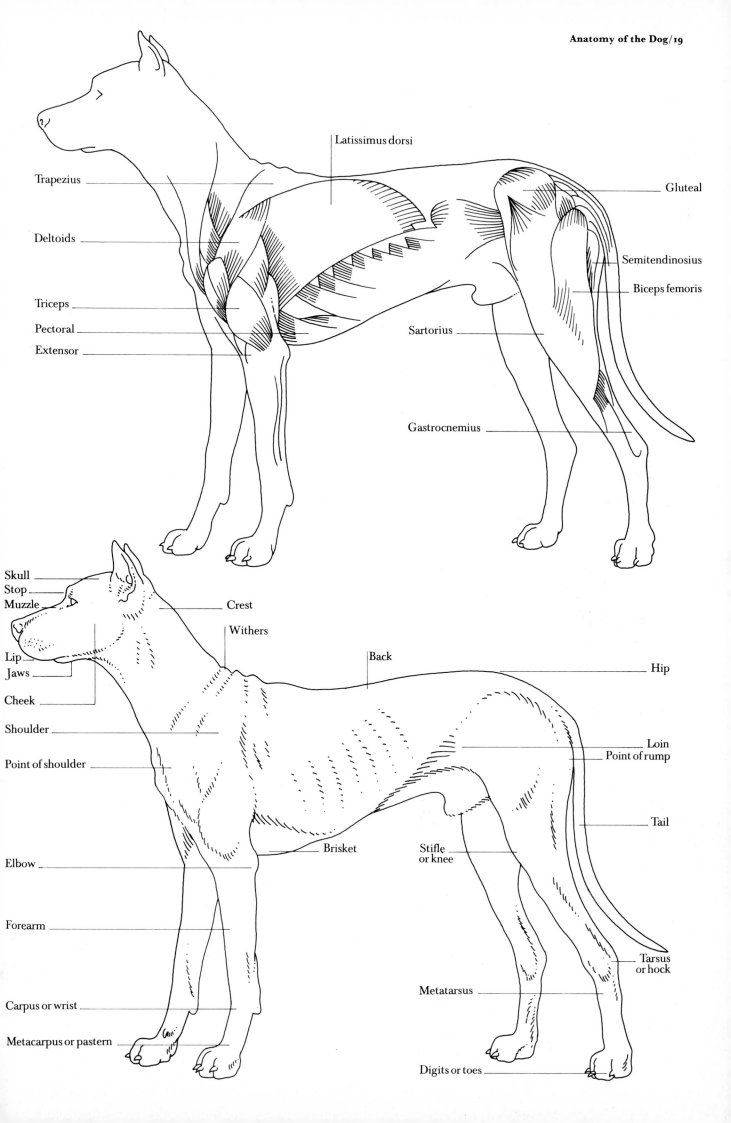

Latissimus dorsi

Trapezius

Gluteal

Deltoids

Semitendinosius

Biceps femoris

Triceps

Pectoral

Sartorius

Extensor

Gastrocnemius

Skull

Stop

Muzzle

Crest

Withers

Lip

Jaws

Back

Hip

Cheek

Shoulder

Point of shoulder

Loin

Point of rump

Elbow

Brisket

Stifle
or knee

Tail

Forearm

Tarsus
or hock

Metatarsus

Carpus or wrist

Metacarpus or pastern

Digits or toes

3 Incisors

1 Canine

4 Premolars

Carnassial tooth

2 Molars

Left: Dentition of the dog.

3 Incisors

1 Canine

4 Premolars

3 Molars

One important variation is the size of the jawbone relative to the width of the skull. Collies, hounds, and terriers, for example, have long jawbones, while short-faced breeds like the Bulldog, Pekingese, and Pug have short jaws. With some of these short-headed breeds the lower jaw is often slightly longer than the upper one. This affects the layout of the dog's teeth (see left) as it is obvious that the long jaws of a dog such as the Greyhound can carry a complete set of teeth more easily than, say, a Pekingese. The normal dog has a total of 42 teeth; the six front ones in the upper and lower jaws are the incisors – biting teeth – and directly behind them are the canines or fangs. Each jaw has two, one on each side. Behind the canines are the premolars and molars – the grinders and crushers. When the upper and lower incisors meet edge to edge, symmetrically, the dog is said to have a 'level

Below: The Irish Setter has strong jaws for retrieving and a soft mouth to avoid hurting its prey. A soft mouth is a sign of a good gundog.

22

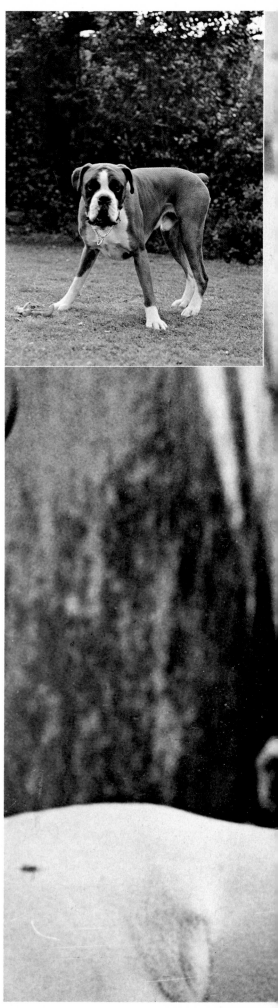

Right: A playful boxer. In
the United States and on the
Continent the ears are cropped
to a point; in England ear
cropping is not permitted.
Far right: On the Continent
the ears of the Great Dane are
cropped to stand at a point, as
in this example. Elsewhere
the tips of the ears are left to
fall forward.

bite,' and a Retriever which carries game
without harming it by biting or tearing is
said to have a 'soft' mouth.

At this point a reference to the practice
of ear cropping (see below) seems appropriate. In some countries ear cropping
is now considered a barbarous custom and
is prohibited. In fact, however, it started
out as a partially humane measure to save
dogs from injury in dogfighting and rat-killing contests. Later it was considered that
many animals actually looked smarter with
cropped ears, so the original purpose was
forgotten and ears were cropped as a
fashionable necessity. Many people are
opposed to this on the grounds that it
inflicts unnecessary pain on young puppies,
and some terrier enthusiasts say that the
shock of the operation has been responsible
for producing terriers which were deficient
in terrier character. Nowadays ear cropping is done under a general anesthetic and
the dog is given tranquilizing drugs.

The dog's nose is a most important component of his anatomy, because his world
is full of scents and he uses it in his everyday
business much as a man uses his eyes.

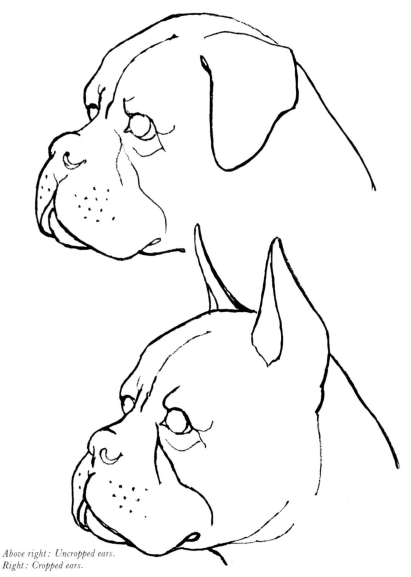

Above right: Uncropped ears.
Right: Cropped ears.

Scenting ability varies with the type of dog. It seems to be most acute in those with a long nose, long ears, and hanging lips, such as hounds and sporting breeds. Shape and color of the nostrils may be important also, since the keenest noses appear to be those when the nostrils are large, black, and wide open. (Exceptions to this color rule are the brown-nosed hunting dogs.) Incidentally, it is a mistake to assume that a cold nose is the sign of a healthy dog. The animal has sweat glands on the nose and if for some reason moisture is leaving the body – as the result of a snooze under blankets or being huddled beside a radiator – the nose will become warm and dry.

The dog's eyes are his most attractive feature, though sight is not one of his strong points. Nor need it be, since his power of hearing and power of scent are so phenomenal. He cannot see colors very well; on the other hand he can differentiate degrees of lightness better than man. He sees motion instantly because, as an animal in the wild, he has had to get his food on the

run. Although he has an eye similar to that of the human, the eye white surrounding the iris or color portion does not show as much. Lids normally cover the white except for a tiny portion at the inner corners. Functionally, a dark eye is no better than a light one. In fact, some gun-dog trainers assert that a yellow-eyed dog sees better than one with dark eyes. But with very few exceptions (of which the Weimaraner is one), dark eyes are preferred in almost every breed. A clear blue eye is known as a 'China' eye, and the dark markings about the eyes of some breeds are termed 'spectacles.'

The normal dog's sense of hearing is extremely acute, and most dogs can hear twice as well as man. Also, although the dog's ear is very much like that of the human, its flap or 'leather' is quite different from the earlap of man. It is made to catch the sound, and it also moves to find the direction from which the sound comes. Selective breeding has evolved a wide variety of earlaps. In some breeds the ear stands erect or 'pricked'; in others, termed 'semipricked,' it rises halfway and then tips slightly forward. In still others it lies flat to the head and is said to be 'dropped.' Pugs have 'buttoned' or 'rose' ears – 'button' ears are turned down though slightly raised at the base, and 'rose' are ears which fold but which are drawn back to expose the inside of the ear (known as the 'burr').

The coat is the dog's complexion, and most dogs have two-ply coats. The long-haired and medium-haired breeds, especially, have an outer coat varying in coarseness over a thick and dense under-coat. Short, smooth-haired dogs have a double coat as well, though it is less notice-able because the undercoat is neither downy nor flat-lying, so it is almost impossible to distinguish between the topcoat and the undercoat. When the undercoat is shed in warm weather, the main change that is observed is the thinner covering of the whole. A 'stand-off' coat is one which stands out from the body, like that of the Chow Chow, while a 'staring' coat is one which is harsh, dry, and ill-conditioned.

Many people feel that the 'docking' or shortening of tails is as abhorrent as the practice of ear cropping. In breeds that are docked the operation is usually carried out when the puppy is about three days old. A skilled hand is needed and the docking should be done only under the supervision of a veterinary surgeon. Normal undocked tails include naturally short tails twisted into screw form like that of the Pug and known as 'screw' tails. 'Ring' or 'ring stern' tails are carried over the back in a near circle, while tails carried high and forward, that is, over the body and parallel to it, are termed 'gay'; 'sickle' and 'saber' tails are, as the terms imply, carried in a semicircle.

Far right: Finnish Spitz puppy. It will maintain a very thick coat in adulthood in order to withstand the cold temperatures of its home country.
Below, both: The tail of the English Springer Spaniel, shown here, is docked for practical, hygenic reasons. Terrier tails are docked to facilitate pulling the dog out of holes without hurting it when it is routing small animals. Pointers, on the other hand, have their tails docked for cosmetic reasons.

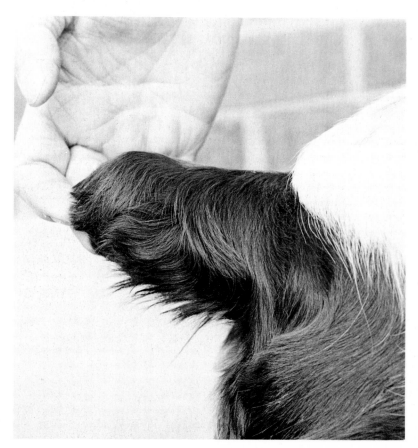

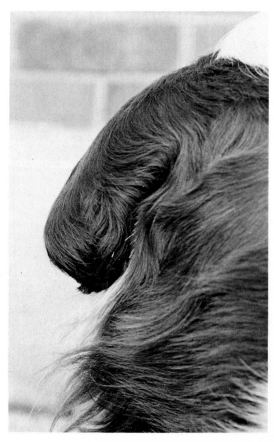

MODERN BREEDS

Below: Ancestors of the dog.

CLASSIFICATION OF BREEDS

There are about 400 breeds of dog in the world, just over 300 of which are registered and recognized by canine organizations. Each breed has a breed standard which outlines its origin, physical characteristics, purpose, and so on, and any number of attempts have been made to classify the breeds into groups based on factors such as physical similarities, common ancestry, or purpose. Unfortunately, however, it has proved impossible to formulate a logical and consistent classification which is universally acceptable, and the result is that different classifications are used in different countries. The Kennel Club of Britain, for example, divides the breeds into six groups: hounds, gundogs, terriers, utility breeds, working breeds, and toys. The American Kennel Club also classifies the breeds into six groups but with certain differences as to which breed belongs to

which group: sporting breeds, hounds, working breeds, terriers, toys, and non-sporting breeds. On the other hand, the system in use in most European countries since 1965 comprises 10 groups – herding breeds, working breeds, terriers, dachshunds, hunting breeds (for large game), hunting breeds (for small game), pointing gun dogs (other than British breeds), British pointing gundogs, other British gundogs, and toys. Since January 1968 yet another classification system has been used at dog shows in the four Scandinavian countries – Denmark, Finland, Norway, and Sweden. This comprises eight groups – spitz breeds, tracking/hunting breeds, gundogs, working breeds/guard dogs, terriers, sight hounds (sporting dogs which hunt by air scent, as distinct from the tracking dogs which hunt primarily by ground scent), nonsporting/companion breeds, and finally toys.

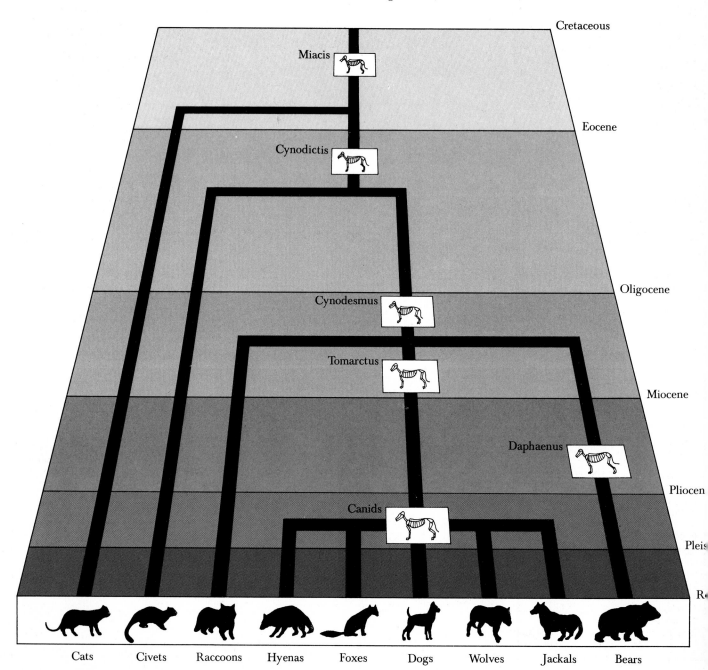

Cretaceous

Miacis

Eocene

Cynodictis

Oligocene

Cynodesmus

Tomarctus

Miocene

Daphaenus

Pliocen

Canids

Pleis

R

Cats   Civets   Raccoons   Hyenas   Foxes   Dogs   Wolves   Jackals   Bears

CLASSIFICATION OF BREEDS (BRITISH)

SPORTING BREEDS

Hound group
Afghan Hounds
Basenjis
Basset Hounds
Basset Griffon Vendeen
Beagles
Bloodhounds
Borzois
Dachshunds (Long-haired)
Dachshunds (Miniature Long-haired)
Dachshunds (Miniature Smooth-haired)
Dachshunds (Miniature Wire-haired)
Dachshunds (Wire-haired)
Deerhounds
Elkhounds
Finnish Spitz
Foxhounds
Greyhounds
Hamiltonstövare
Ibizan Hounds
Irish Wolfhounds
Otter Hounds
Pharaoh Hounds
Rhodesian Ridgebacks
Salukis
Swiss Laufhunds (Jura)
Whippets

Gundog group
American Cocker Spaniels
Chesapeake Bay Retrievers
Clumber Spaniels
Cocker Spaniels
Curly-coated Retrievers
English Setters
English Springer Spaniels
Field Spaniels
Flat-coated Retrievers
German Long-haired Pointers
German Short-haired Pointers
German Wire-haired Pointers
Golden Retrievers
Gordon Setters
Hungarian Vizslas
Irish Setters
Irish Water Spaniels
Italian Spinones
Labroador Retrievers
Large Münsterländers
Pointers
Small Münsterländers
Sussex Spaniels
Weimaraners
Welsh Springer Spaniels
Wire-haired Pointing Griffons

Terrier group
Airedale Terriers
Australian Terriers
Bedlington Terriers
Border Terriers
Bull Terriers
Cairn Terriers
Dandie Dinmont Terriers
Glen of Imaal Terriers
Irish Terriers
Kerry Blue Terriers
Lakeland Terriers
Manchester Terriers
Miniature Bull Terriers
Norfolk Terriers
Norwich Terriers
Scottish Terriers
Sealyham Terriers
Skye Terriers
Smooth Fox Terriers
Soft-coated Wheaten Terriers
Staffordshire Bull Terriers
Welsh Terriers
West Highland Terriers
Wire Fox Terriers

NONSPORTING BREEDS

Utility Group
Boston Terriers
Bulldogs
Canaan Dogs
Chow Chows
Dalmatians
French Bulldogs
Giant Schnauzers
Iceland Dogs
Japanese Akitas
Keeshonds
Leonbergers
Lhasa Apsos
Mexican Hairless
Miniature Schnauzers
Poodles (Miniature)
Poodles (Standard)
Poodles (Toy)
Schipperkes
Schnauzers
Shih Tzus
Tibetan Spaniels
Tibetan Terriers

Working group
Alaskan Malamutes
Anatolian (Karabesh) Dogs
Australian Cattle Dogs
Bearded Collies
Beaucerons
Belgian Shepherd Dogs (Groenendaels)
Belgian Shepherd Dogs (Lakenois)
Belgian Shepherd Dogs (Malinois)
Belgian Shepherd Dogs (Tervuerens)
Bernese Mountain Dogs
Border Collies
Bouvier de Flandres
Boxers
Briards
Bullmastiffs
Dobermanns
Eskimo Dogs
Estrela Mountain Dogs
German Shepherd Dogs (Alsatians)
Great Danes
Hungarian Kuvasz
Hungarian Pulis
Maremma Italian Sheepdogs
Mastiffs
Neapolitan Mastiffs
Newfoundlands
Norwegian Buhunds
Old English Sheepdogs
Polish Sheepdogs
Portuguese Water Dogs
Pyrenean Mountain Dogs
Pyrenean Sheepdogs
Rottweilers
Rough Collies
St Bernards
Samoyeds
Shetland Sheepdogs
Siberian Huskies
Smooth Collies
Tibetan Mastiffs
Welsh Corgis, Cardigan
Welsh Corgis, Pembroke

Toy group
Affenpinschers
Bichons Frisés
Cavalier King Charles Spaniels
Chihuahuas (Long Coat)
Chihuahuas (Smooth Coat)
Chinese Crested Dogs
English Toy Terriers (Black and Tan)
Griffons Bruxellois
Italian Greyhounds
Japanese Chin
King Charles Spaniels
Löwchen
Maltese
Miniature Pinschers
Papillons
Pekingese
Pomeranians
Pugs
Silky Terriers
Yorkshire Terriers

CLASSIFICATION OF BREEDS (AMERICAN)

Sporting Group
American Water Spaniels
Brittany Spaniels
Chesapeake Bay Retrievers
Clumber Spaniels
Cocker Spaniels
Curly-coated Retrievers
English Cocker Spaniels
English Setters
English Springer Spaniels
Field Spaniels
Flat-coated Retrievers
German Short-haired Pointers
German Wire-haired Pointers
Golden Retrievers
Gordon Setters
Irish Setters
Irish Water Spaniels
Labrador Retrievers
Pointers
Sussex Spaniels
Vizslas
Weimaraners
Welsh Springer Spaniels
Wire-haired Pointing Griffons

Hound group
Afghan Hounds
American Foxhounds
Basenjis
Basset Hounds
Beagles
Black and Tan Coonhounds
Bloodhounds
Borzois
Dachshunds
English Foxhounds
Greyhounds
Harriers
Ibizan Hounds
Irish Wolfhounds
Norwegian Elkhounds
Otter Hounds
Rhodesian Ridgebacks
Salukis
Scottish Deerhounds
Whippets

Working group
Akitas
Alaskan Malamutes
Bearded Collies
Belgian Malinois
Belgian Sheepdogs
Belgian Terveuren
Bernese Mountain Dogs
Bouviers de Flandres
Boxers
Briards
Bullmastiffs
Collies
Dobermann Pinschers
German Shepherd Dogs
Giant Schnauzers
Great Danes
Great Pyrenees (Pyrenean Mountain Dog)
Komondor
Kuvasz
Mastiffs
Newfoundlands
Old English Sheepdogs
Puli
Rottweilers
St Bernards
Samoyeds
Shetland Sheepdogs
Siberian Huskies
Standard Schnauzers
Welsh Corgis, Cardigan
Welsh Corgis, Pembroke

Terrier group
Airedale Terriers
American Staffordshire Terriers
Australian Terriers
Bedlington Terriers
Border Terriers
Bull Terriers
Cairn Terriers
Dandie Dinmont Terriers
Fox Terriers
Irish Terriers
Kerry Blue Terriers
Lakeland Terriers
Manchester Terriers
Miniature Schnauzers
Norfolk Terriers
Norwich Terriers
Scottish Terriers
Sealyham Terriers
Skye Terriers
Soft-coated Wheaten Terriers
Staffordshire Bull Terriers
Welsh Terriers
West Highland White Terriers

Toy group
Affenpinschers
Brussels Griffons
Chihuahuas
English Toy Spaniels
Italian Greyhounds
Japanese Chin
Maltese
Manchester Terriers
Miniature Pinschers
Papillons
Pekingese
Pomeranians
Poodles (Toy)
Pugs
Shih Tzus
Silky Terriers
Yorkshire Terriers

Nonsporting group
Bichons Frisés
Boston Terriers
Bulldogs
Chow Chows
Dalmatians
French Bulldogs
Keeshonds
Lhasa Apsos
Poodles
Schipperkes
Tibetan Terriers

The hound group

Dogs in this group were developed for sporting purposes and most of them are used primarily to trail game by ground scents. They include the Afghan Hound, Basenji, Basset Hound, Beagle, Bloodhound, Dachshund, American Foxhound, English Foxhound, Greyhound, Harrier, Norwegian Elkhound, Otter Hound, Saluki, and Whippet. The hound group also includes the Irish Wolfhound, Borzoi, and Scottish Deerhound, all of which hunt large game primarily by sight.

The typical hound breeds are powerfully

built dogs with sturdy legs, long heads and muzzles, pendulous ears and pendulous upper lips or 'flews.' The Bloodhound, which exhibits these characteristics in an exaggerated form, has the keenest nose for scents of all dogs but it is heavily built and slow. Because of this the Bloodhound has virtually ceased to be a sporting dog and is now used almost exclusively by the police authorities to trail criminals and missing persons.

In the United States the two most popular hounds are the Beagle and the Dachshund. Basically, both breeds are

Right: The Beagle is most often kept as a pet, but is also used for hunting hare and rabbits on foot. Beagles have good noses and prefer being outdoors following scents.
Below: The Basset Hound is trained to hunt with its nose, but it is not particularly fast.

hunting dogs and the Beagle's popularity is due to the fact that thousands of rural sportsmen use them for hunting rabbits. Dogs of the Dachshund type are known to have existed in Egypt in the fifteenth century BC. Three thousand years later, in the fifteenth century AD, Englishmen, Germans, and Italians had similar dogs, but it was in Germany that the *dackel* developed its modern shape. In the United States the Dachshund is rarely used for hunting and its popularity stems from the fact that it is a small, intelligent, and friendly pet.

Left: An African breed of ancient origins, the Basenji is used in its homeland for hunting and tracking. As a pet it is intelligent and obedient.
Below left: An adult Bloodhound with a puppy. The Bloodhound is a hardy dog which will track scents to their source for miles.

34

The gundog/sporting group

Sometimes known as the 'sporting' group, the gundog breeds include the varieties of pointers, retrievers, setters, spaniels, and the Weimaraner. Dogs in this group track by air scent and act as hunters' aides, finding and retrieving small game and birds. Spaniels are the largest class of hunting breeds, and it would seem that the Irish used them first, although the name spaniel suggests that they originated in Spain. English literature of the fourteenth century mentions 'spanyells' and they were used in falconry during the sixteenth century – probably to retrieve game killed or injured by the falcons. The spaniel family is divided into those breeds which hunt and retrieve only, and toy spaniels which do not hunt. Most of the sporting spaniels operate close to the hunter, ranging back and forth flushing out game for the sportsman to shoot. Having flushed the game, a well-trained spaniel will then sit until ordered to find the dead bird or animal and fetch it back to the hunter.

A second group of gundogs includes the pointers and setters which hunt game birds by pointing. Unlike the spaniels which operate close to the sportsman, the pointing breeds range well ahead – often out of sight. When they scent game they do not flush it immediately but stand immobile a few meters away, with their noses pointing toward it. They remain in this position until the hunter flushes and

Right: A group of German Short-haired Pointers playing. This dog is an excellent and persevering hunter which will point and retrieve game, both on land and in water.
Below: The Springer Spaniel works by flushing out small game and then retrieving it.

shoots the bird or birds. A well-trained pointer will hold a point for up to two hours, standing quietly until the game is shot and the order to find and retrieve is given.

Pointers are of comparatively recent origin, their development moving with the development of sporting guns. The English Setter and the Red Irish Setter are among the most popular of these so-called 'bird dogs.'

The retrievers are hunting specialists. Their job is to locate game which has been killed or wounded by the hunter and to bring it to their masters. During the hunting of upland game, retrievers are often worked with spaniels. The spaniels quarter the ground and 'spring' the game, but the retrievers remain with the hunter until the quarry is downed; only then is the retriever sent out to do his job. The most popular retriever breeds include the Labrador, Chesapeake Bay, Golden Retriever, and the Irish Water Spaniel.

The Curly-coated Retriever at work. This sporting gundog is a good swimmer and is quite happy to retrieve downed quarry from the water, which he holds gently and clear of the water. The distinctive coat is water repellent.

The terriers

The name terrier is derived from the Latin *terra*, earth. They are so-called because they hunt by digging into the earth to rout out furry animals such as badgers, otters, marmots, and the like. In some cases their duty is merely to force their quarry from its den to allow the hunter to capture it. In other cases the terrier's job is to find and destroy the animals, either on the surface or underground.

The terrier group includes breeds which differ so profoundly from each other that the extreme types appear to have little in common. For example, the Bull Terrier (which is related to the Mastiff) bears little resemblance to the Airedale Terrier (whose predecessors were, in fact, Otter Hounds crossed with terriers of the Aire Valley). England, Ireland, and Scotland have produced most of the terrier breeds, but the Sealyham and – as their name implies – the Welsh Terriers originated in Wales. Germany has produced Schnauzers and there are Tibetan (Lhasa) Terriers.

This Long-haired Norfolk Terrier has drop ears instead of the Norwich's prick ears.

An Airedale puppy. This type of terrier is the largest of the group, which traditionally rout and kill small mammals.

Airedales have strong noses good for all-round hunting, but they are also good working dogs and reliable pets.

The working group

This group – which includes sheepdogs, the Bernese Mountain Dog, the Boxer, the Bullmastiff, the Collie, the Dobermann Pinscher, German Shepherd (often called Alsatian), Great Dane, the Puli, Rottweiler, the Samoyed, the Siberian Husky, the St Bernard, and Welsh Corgis – has the greatest utilitarian value of all the modern canine classifications. They are not normally regarded as sporting dogs, but are employed as cattle herders, draft animals, guides for the blind, and as police assistants.

The German Shepherd, Boxer, Dobermann Pinscher, Rottweiler, Great Dane, and Giant Schnauzer are all in the police group, as these breeds are trained as sentries and guard dogs. (The Airedale and the Standard Schnauzer from the terrier group are also trained for the same role, and Bloodhounds from the hound group are often used by the police for tracking duties, so all of these breeds may be considered 'police dogs' – a term often mistakenly used solely to denote the German Shepherd.)

Other breeds in the working group were developed as farmers' assistants. These include the Collie from Scotland, the Puli from Hungary, the Corgi from Wales, the Old English Sheepdog, the Shetland Sheepdog, the Belgian Sheepdog, and the German Shepherd – all of which are herders. The Norwegian Elkhound from the hound group is also used for herding duties. (In America the dog most commonly used for herding work on farms is an unrecognized breed unofficially called the American Shepherd. It is a Collie type but has a shorter muzzle and smaller body than the English Border Collie – which is also a breed not officially recognized.)

Draft animals are also included in the utility group of working dogs, the best known of these being the Eskimo and Alaskan Malamutes which are used to pull sledges.

A further division of working dogs comprises the 'rescue' breeds – the St Bernard and the Newfoundland. The former breed is best known for work in the Swiss Alps and is popularly associated with a small cask of brandy slung below the collar. The Newfoundland, which is a powerful swimmer, is used to carry lifelines to stricken vessels and to help rescue the survivors of shipwrecks.

Finally, the guide dogs for the blind, the guard dogs, and war dogs may be considered perhaps the most important of the working breeds, and these are discussed on p. 213–17.

Right: A German Shepherd exercising shows the strength and speed with which this dog can move. It is a very loyal and trainable dog, making it particularly suitable for use as a police dog, guard dog, or guide dog.
Below: The West Siberian Laika (center) is not well known outside the Soviet Union, where it is a hardy working dog. Beside it are two Gontjaja harnessed up for hauling a sledge.
Bottom: The Siberian Husky, a powerful and fast sledge dog, is a very hard worker, but has become popular as a pet over the years.

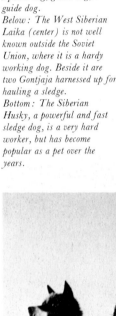

The toy group

All the dogs in the groups already described, that is, the hounds, the gundogs, the terriers, and the 'working' dogs, were bred originally for a specific purpose – for hunting, for tracking, to rout out vermin, to protect livestock or people, or to fill some other need. But the vast majority of dogs are, in fact, kept primarily as pets and, even if they are suited to a utilitarian role, many of them never fulfill it. Thousands of spaniels never learn to hunt and retrieve, thousands of sheepdogs are never used to herd livestock, and comparatively few of the breeds developed for police work or as guide dogs are ever employed in such a role; most modern domesticated dogs are kept simply as companions and pets.

The dogs of the toy group are generally regarded as ideal house pets, earning their keep by providing friendly companionship, although most of them develop a protective instinct which results in their becoming effective sentries, warning their masters of approaching strangers. As their name implies, all the toy dogs are small – ranging from the tiny Chihuahuas to Pugs. Most toy breeds are miniature counterparts of larger breeds. For example, in appearance and shape the English toy spaniels and Japanese spaniels resemble the hunting spaniels, and the Italian Greyhound is a dwarfed version of the ancient Greyhound.

Above right: The Italian Greyhound is a very popular and gentle toy dog, which has been bred from large Greyhounds to obtain a miniature breed.
Below: The Affenpinscher is a perfect house dog because it is happy in small areas.
Right: The Shih Tzu is bred strictly as a house dog, and makes a very affectionate companion.

*Above : Blenheim Cavalier
King Charles Spaniels. This
toy breed provides very lively
and loyal family pets.*
*Right : Like all toy dogs, the
Bichon Frisé was bred as a
lapdog, originally in France
and Belgium, and is a
pleasant dog around the house.
The adults require a fair
amount of grooming.*

The miscellaneous group

This group comprises a miscellany of eight nonsporting breeds – Boston Terriers, English and French Bulldogs, Chow Chows, Dalmatians, Keeshonds, Poodles, and Schipperkes. The Chow Chow is probably the oldest of the breeds in the group, and it is popular in England and the United States as a companion and guard dog. The Boston Terrier is one of the few breeds developed in the United States.

Wild dogs

Finally, in classifying dogs the undomesticated animals deserve a brief mention. Apart from wolves and jackals there are a number of other wild dogs. The Australian Dingo or Warrigal, which resembles the

Below: This championship Standard Poodle is in peak condition. The Poodle breed is extremely intelligent and friendly, and thus very popular as pets, especially in the United States.

German Shepherd in size and build, is a menace to Australian livestock. But the Dingo can be domesticated and they are sometimes used by the Australian aborigines as hunting dogs. The Indian Dhole is the Asiatic equivalent of the Dingo, which it closely resembles. Unlike the Dingo, however, it does not take to domesticity and packs of Dholes are very destructive to game. In Africa the wild dog is known as the African Hunting Dog or Hyena Dog. Its coat is blotched yellow, black, and white like that of a hyena and its large upstanding ears are its main characteristic. Like the Dholes these dogs hunt in packs, preying chiefly on antelopes; also like the Dholes wild dogs cannot be domesticated.

Below: The Boston Terrier is a very playful and energetic animal, particularly popular in the United States where the breed was developed. It is a good pet, but also likes the companionship of other Boston Terriers.

DICTIONARY OF DOGS

The descriptions of individual breeds which follow are presented in alphabetical order according to the names by which they are most commonly referred (the country of origin is given at the head of the text after the name).

Above: Affenpinscher, originally bred in Germany as a ratting dog.
Right: Short-haired Afghan Hound.
Far right: A very decorative and elegant looking Long-haired Afghan Hound.

Affenpinscher *Germany*

The Affenpinscher, which resembles a monkey, is a very old breed and was depicted by Dutch painters in the fourteenth century. It has always been regarded as a close relative of the more common smooth-haired Miniature Pinscher and at one time was even considered to be a wire-haired variety of that breed.

Its monkey-like appearance is due largely to its round, black, lustrous eyes. It is a sturdy little dog with a rounded skull, an undershot mouth, small pointed ears, a docked tail, and a wiry coat.

The color is generally black, but black with tan or gray markings is also found, as are other colors except very light ones.

Afghan Hound *Afghanistan*

The Afghan Hound is distinguished by its long silky coat, its springy gait, and aristocratic, albeit somewhat bizarre, bearing. It probably originated in the Middle East but subsequently became established in the bleak and rugged countryside of northern Afghanistan. There it was used for hunting. The Afghan is dignified and carries himself with aloofness. The head is long, the jaws especially so, and the eyes are preferably dark. The coat is long and fine in texture, with a silky topknot on the head; the tail curls into a characteristic ring at the end. Afghans come in all shades of brown, in black, and black and brown, and they are extremely popular all over the world.

Previous page, left: The Afghan Hound is a very strong and dignified dog capable of great speed as a racer.
Previous page, right: The Cavalier King Charles Spaniel is closely related to the King Charles Spaniel but has surpassed it in popularity.

Airedale Terrier *Britain*

Because of its size the Airedale is unique within the terrier group, which is comprised mainly of active little dogs used for going to earth after a fox, a badger, or similar quarry. It is unlikely that the Airedale has ever been employed below ground. It is largely a descendant of the black and tan hunting terriers, now extinct, which were crossed with foxhounds in the Airedale Valley in Yorkshire. This cross-breeding resulted in a dog which combined the stubbornness and courage of the terrier with the good nose and hunting instinct of the hound. At the turn of the century some Airedales were sent to Germany where they were used first to pull small carts, and later as guard dogs, police dogs, and finally, in World War I, as war dogs.

The Airedale is a terrier in temperament and elegant in appearance. The head is long with a flat skull, flat cheeks, and very powerful jaws and teeth. The eyes are small, dark brown, and full of terrier expression in combination with calm confidence. The coat is hard and wiry with a soft undercoat. Left untended for too long, Airedales rapidly grow into woolly bears. The ears are small and folded, and carried to the side of the head.

The color on the head and legs is a warm tan, with black or dark grizzle on the rest of the body. Dogs stand about 24 inches at the shoulder, slightly less for bitches. The weight is usually around 55 pounds.

Akita, see Japanese Akita

Alaskan Malamute *Alaska*

The Alaskan Malamute is one of the Arctic spitz breeds named after the Eskimo group which is supposed to have developed the breed. It was used originally as a sledge dog by the Alaskans, and it is in fact the largest of the sledge-dog breeds. In the summer months the Malamute was employed as a pack animal. At the turn of the century Alaskan Malamutes attracted the attention of the white man, and after World War II large numbers were imported to Canada and the United States.

The Alaskan Malamute is a big, powerful, energetic dog which carries its head proudly. The eyes are set obliquely and resemble those of a wolf, but having a friendly expression. The coat is thick and coarse, particularly abundant on the chest, neck, and tail, where it forms a plume.

The color is usually gray or black with white marking. Dogs stand 25 to 28 inches at the shoulder, bitches 23 to 25 inches.

Right: Airedale Terrier.
Far right: Alaskan Malamute.

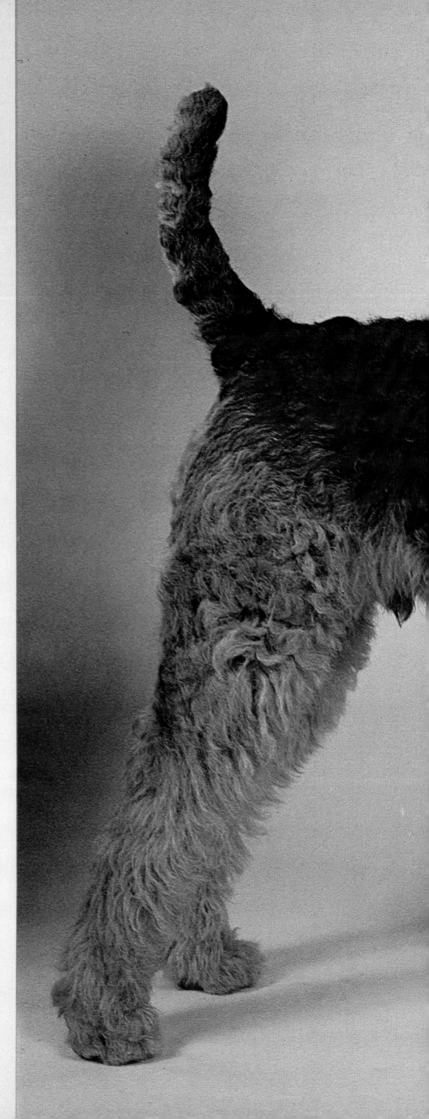

Alpine Mastiff and Alpine Spaniel
Switzerland

'Alpine Mastiff' was the name given to the breed now known as St Bernard. It is thought that 'Alpine Spaniel' may also have once applied to the St Bernard, although it is more likely that it referred to a smaller breed of dog resembling the modern Clumber Spaniel.

Alsatian, see German Shepherd

American Cocker Spaniel *USA*

The American Cocker Spaniel is an interesting example of what can happen when a breed moves from one country to another. When the British began to colonize America they introduced spaniels which gradually, and without any mixture of strange blood, managed to become so different and 'American' in type that, toward the end of the last century, they were eventually officially recognized as a separate breed. This more extreme and showy spaniel variety has been popular as a pet for a long time in America and in recent years it has gained ground in Britain and Scandinavia.

The American Cocker Spaniel is usually slightly smaller than the English variety. Its coat, which is either straight or wavy, is much more profuse than that of the ordinary Cocker, especially on the ears, legs, and belly. The color varies from black, black and tan, and particolors or roans.

American Coonhound *USA*

This black and tan Coonhound is the only one of the six varieties of Coonhound officially recognized as a breed by the American Kennel Club. It is used primarily for hunting raccoon and opossum. As distinct from the other Coonhounds, it is a close relative of the English Bloodhound, though it also has unmistakable traces of the American Foxhound. Although it resembles a Bloodhound, the American Coonhound is of lighter build and it lacks the folds of loose skin on the forehead. The ears are low set, long, and pendulous.

American Foxhound *USA*

The main difference between the American Foxhound and its English counterpart (see *English Foxhound*) is its size, for it is generally much bigger. Originally the two breeds were used for similar purposes, but while the Foxhound is never shown at ordinary dog shows in Britain, the American Foxhound is a popular dog in the United States. In comparison with the English breed the American Foxhound is a far more imposing and longer-legged dog. The ears are large, the body is strong and well built, and the tail is carried straight up. All colors are acceptable. Height at the shoulder is usually just over 24 inches.

American Toy Terrier *USA*

The American Toy Terrier is not officially recognized as a separate breed. Despite this, it is very popular as a pet. It is descended from the Fox Terrier but its forebears incorporated various toy breeds.

The American Toy Terrier resembles a small Smooth Fox Terrier but is much finer in bone and has pricked ears. The head is more pointed and the jaws weaker. The tail, docked short, is carried erect.

The color is usually white, with black or black and tan markings. A typical example should not exceed 8 to 9 pounds in weight.

American Water Spaniel *USA*

The American relative of the Irish Water Spaniel is considerably smaller than its ancestor. Its exact origin in unknown, but it is thought that the Irish Water Spaniel was crossed with smaller American spaniel breeds. In the United States it is sometimes known as the Boykin Spaniel after a town in South Carolina. Two or three hundred puppies are registered yearly in the United States, but the breed is almost unknown outside its home country. It was not officially recognized until 1940.

In the main, the breed is a smaller copy of its Irish relative. It is, however, slightly longer in body and has a broader skull. Its tail is covered with hair right to the tip. The coat is tightly curled.

The color is liver or chocolate brown; small white markings on the toes and chest are acceptable. Height at the shoulder is 15 to 18 inches.

Australian Cattle Dog *Australia*

The Australian Cattle Dog, previously known as the 'heeler,' is considered to be a cross between the Collie, Kelpie, and Dingo. Be that as it may, the fact that the breed earns its keep herding cattle is beyond doubt. It is an extremely efficient worker, alert and keen, and is therefore used to herd cattle rather than sheep. The nickname 'heeler' was acquired because of its habit of quietly circling the herd and then, when necessary, racing in to nip the hocks of any stragglers.

The Australian Cattle Dog is light, agile, and active. The head is broad with a slightly domed skull and gradually tapering foreface. The ears are pointed, carried erect at a slight angle. The eyes are dark, oval in shape, with an alert expression. The nose is black. The body is of moderate length and strongly built. The front legs

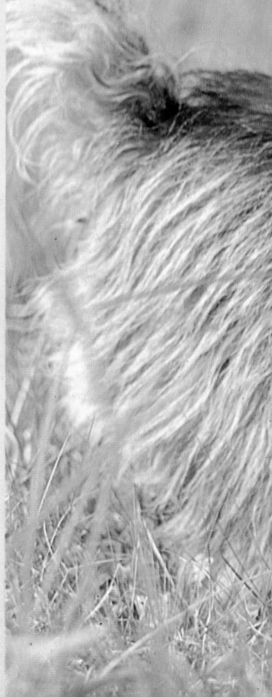

Above: Australian Cattle Dogs.
Right: Australian Terrier.

are straight with slightly sloping pasterns; hindquarters have hocks well let down. The tail reaches the hock, is well covered with hair and carried in a gentle upward curve. The coat is fairly short and rough with a soft, thick undercoat.

The color is usually a mottled blue with or without black markings. The head is blue or black and tan, and the tan should extend to markings on the forelegs, brisket, and on the inside of the thighs. The color may also be red speckled with rich red markings on the head. Height at the shoulder is about 18 inches.

Australian Terrier *Australia*
Australia is a country of strange animals: kangaroos, wallabies, koala bears, and the talking budgerigar. In its own way the Australian Terrier is equally strange, yet its roots are wholly British. Before World War II Australian immigrants came mostly from the United Kingdom and they took their terriers with them. These dogs, all different varieties, eventually produced the conglomerate out of which the Australian Terrier breed was born. (It is not known exactly which terrier breeds were involved but there is no doubt that the Yorkshire played a leading role.)

The Australian Terrier is a rather low-set, active little dog, with a keen expression in its dark eyes. The ears are small, pricked, or dropped forward. The neck has a decided frill of longer hair.

The color is dark blue or silver gray with rich tan markings on the head and the legs. Height at the shoulder is about 10 inches and the weight about 10 to 11 pounds (Britain), 12 to 14 pounds (USA).

Basenji *Central Africa*

The Basenji is an unusual – some say unique – member of the spitz breeds. Although they are comparatively new to the Western world, Basenjis have long been known in Central Africa, where they are used mainly for hunting and tracking game. In Europe it is now well established as a pet, and is popular as such because, unlike most of the other Spitz breeds, it does not make a nuisance of itself by excessive yapping. The Basenji cannot bark and the only noise it can make is a chortling yodel. Its other distinguishing feature is its cleanliness; to clean itself a Basenji behaves almost like a cat.

The Basenji is a lively and graceful animal, finely boned. The head is characterized by dark eyes, wrinkled forehead, and pointed ears. The tail is set high and tightly curled close to the thigh. The skin is very supple, the coat sleek and close.

The color is usually pure chestnut and white, but sometimes tricolor. The height at the shoulder for dogs is about 17 inches, and about 16 inches for bitches. The weight is around 20 pounds.

Basset Hound *Britain*

With its Bloodhound-type head on a short-legged, long and heavily built body, and its long tail, the Basset Hound presents a stolid, somewhat bizarre appearance. But it has a gentle temperament and has become a very popular pet in Britain.

The Basset was used originally in France and Belgium for hunting deer, hares, and rabbits. In Britain it was crossed with the Bloodhound, from which it acquired the typical head and the Bloodhound's extraordinary scenting powers. Its most prominent characteristics are a soulful expression, loose skin, and long, low shape. The coat is smooth and short.

Any recognized hound color is acceptable, but generally it is tricolor (black, white, and tan) or lemon and white. The height at the shoulder is about 20 inches for inches, and weight about 44 pounds.

Bavarian Gebirgsschweisshund *Germany*

The Bavarian Gebirgsschweisshund is a lightly built hunting dog with a sensitive nose used for tracking deer in the Bavarian alps. It is related to the Hanoverian Schweisshund, which it strongly resembles. Both dogs count the Swedish Drever and the Dachshund among their ancestors. The height at the shoulder is about 20 inches for dogs, 18 inches for bitches.

Above: Basset Hound.
Right: Basenji.

Beagle *Britain*

Compared with the Foxhound, which is rarely seen at the dog shows these days, the rise in popularity of the Beagle has been meteoric and universal. Yet the Beagle has much in common with the Foxhound, which, like the Beagle, is a hunting dog. Used singly, in pairs, or in packs with the huntsmen usually on foot, Beagles are employed to track hares in Britain and the cottontail rabbit in the United States. In Britain, and increasingly in other parts of the world, Beagles are kept mostly as pets. (Mention should also be made of the fact that, because of their small size and uniform weight, Beagles have also become the most popular dogs for laboratory and medical research in the United States.) In some tropical countries, such as Sri Lanka and Venezuela, packs of Beagles are also used for hunting leopard.

The Beagle is sturdy and of a compact build, giving the impression of great stamina and energy. The head is powerful without being coarse, the skull domed with a well-defined stop (the angle between the forehead and the muzzle,) the nose broad, and the ears long and fine in texture. The neck is moderately long, well set into a noticeably ribbed, muscular body. The legs are straight, of good substance, round in bone, and with well-knuckled, strongly padded feet. The tail is carried gaily but not curled over the back. As well as the smooth-coated Beagle, which has a short and very close coat, there is also a less common rough-coated variety, which has dense wiry hair.

The color varies, but any recognized hound color – which usually includes some white – is acceptable. The height at the shoulder is 12 to 16 inches.

Left: Beagle.

Bearded Collie *Britain*

All Collies hail from Scotland. The name derives from the old Anglo-Saxon word Col, meaning black. In Scotland the sheep were usually black in color and so were called 'Colleys,' and the dogs that worked them were known simply as Colley Dogs. In the course of time this was shortened to 'Collies.'

Bearded Collies were known before the twentieth century as the Highland Collie, when they were purely working dogs in the Scottish Highlands. Nowadays they are more often the glamorous pets of the fashionable set. The Bearded Collie is active and strongly built without the massive appearance of the Old English Sheepdog and, above all, without the enormous coat of the latter. The coat is profuse and shaggy without being too thick, and is particularly abundant around the eyes and foreface.

The color is slate or sandy with or without white. The height at the shoulder is 20 to 24 inches for dogs, 18 to 22 inches for bitches.

Below: Bearded Collies.

Bedlington Terrier *Britain*

The Bedlington is essentially a wholly British terrier, whose forbears probably came from Northumberland. Opinions differ as to whether the Dandie Dinmont contributed to the development of the Bedlington breed or vice versa, but the early specimens of both breeds are said to have had much in common.

In the early part of the nineteenth century, Bedlingtons were used primarily to go to ground in search of vermin. With the passage of time they were increasingly employed on the surface to catch rabbits. To cater for this new use the old Bedlington was crossed with the Whippet and the shape and outline of the original breed changed, the stubby legs becoming longer and the frame taking on a more stream-lined look. The result combined the merits of terrier and hound coupled with a gentle pleasant dispostion. Yet, Bedlingtons have never been really popular as pets.

The Bedlington is a graceful, muscular dog with a pear-shaped head and roach-back. The head and skull are narrow, the jaw long and tapering with no stop. The nose should be black for blues and tans, brown for livers and sandy colors, with small, bright eyes – dark for blues, light for livers and sandies. The tail should be thick, tapering, and gracefully curved. Colors are blue, blue and tan, liver, or sandy. The height for dogs is 16 inches, bitches 15 inches. The weight is 17 to 25 pounds.

Belgian Malinois *Belgium*

The Belgian Malinois, which takes its name from the town of Malines, is a variety of sheepdog known in Belgium as the Chien Berger Belge Malinois. The main difference between it and its two relatives, the Tervueren and the Groenendael, is the coat and, in the latter case, the color. The Malinois is of the same type as its relatives and was used as a sheepdog to about the same extent in its home country. The texture of its coat is, however, much more like that of a German Shepherd than its longer-coated relatives. All three varieties of Belgian Sheepdog have the same marked aversion to moving in a straight line and instead tend to move in circles.

The Malinois and the Tervueren are the same color; the coat varies from fawn to mahogany with black tips, slightly lighter on the dog's underside. White is only acceptable on the toes, as is a small white spot on the chest. The height at the shoulder is 24 to 26 inches for dogs, 22 to 24 inches for bitches.

Right: Bedlington Terrier.

Belgian Shepherd *Belgium*

An important variety of Belgian Sheepdog is the Groenendael, which looks rather
like a black German Shepherd although it
has a slightly lighter and taller build.

Like the Malinois and the Tervueren,
the Groenendael is a herding breed which
has guarded sheep in Belgium from time
immemorial. It was not until the turn of the
century, however, that the classification
was introduced which made them into
breeds in the modern sense. The Belgian
police force has used Groenendaels for
many years, but elsewhere they are kept
primarily as companions and pets.

The Groenendael has an alert and
attentive expression, a pointed foreface,
and eyes which vary in color from amber
to brown. Its coat forms a mane round the
neck and its tail is bushy. One peculiarity of
the breed is that it prefers running in a
circle rather than in a straight line.

The color is black. The height at the
shoulder is 24 to 26 inches for dogs, 22 to 24
inches for bitches. See also *Laekenois*.

Belgian Tervueren *Belgium*

The characteristics and appearance of the
Belgian Tervueren are very similar to
those of the Belgian Sheepdog. Like the
Groenendael, to which it is closely related,
the Tervueren resembles a light, lanky
German Shepherd although there is little
trace of that breed in its pedigree.

About the turn of the century there
existed in Belgium a black sheepdog which,
mated to a similarly black sheepdog bitch,
produced the breed now known as the
Groenendael. Previously, however, the
same dog had been mated to another bitch,
which was brown with black shadings, and
the resulting litter became the ancestors of
the Tervueren. The breed differs from the
Groenendael chiefly in color – brown with
black tips to the coat. The height at the
shoulder is 24 to 26 inches for dogs, 22 to 25
inches for bitches.

Both breeds, which are fairly rare outside Belgium, take their names from the
Belgian villages near Brussels from which
they are thought to have originated.

Above: Groendendael.
Right: Belgian Tervueren.

Berger de la Brie *France*

The Berger or Chien de la Brie, sometimes known as the Briard, is descended from the sheepdogs which accompanied the Asian armies that invaded Europe after the fall of the Roman Empire. (These breeds included the Hungarian Komondor, Kuvasz and Puli, and the Russian Owcharka.) The modern Briard is an excellent sheepdog; in World War I the French Army used Briards as war dogs to carry ammunition, first aid equipment, and small loads to isolated sections of the front.

The Briard is tall with a long and shaggy coat. The head has a marked stop and the ears are cropped and heavily fringed. The long tail is carried low, the fringes forming a plume.

All colors are acceptable, but a dark, blackish gray is usually preferred. The height at the shoulder is 24 to 27 inches for dogs, 22 to 25 inches for bitches.

Bernese Mountain Dog *Switzerland*

The Bernese Mountain Dog was hardly known outside Switzerland until quite recently and it has now exchanged the role of sheepdog for family pet. It bears an unmistakable resemblance to the St Bernard, but, although they have a common origin, the Bernese Mountain Dog has existed as an independent breed for as long as its larger relative.

In size and general outline the Bernese Mountain Dog is not unlike the Golden Retriever. It is strong and agile and moves like a Scotch Collie. The head is broad, the eyes dark brown, and the ears carried close to the head. The coat is profuse, close, and fairly soft.

Above: Berger de la Brie, or Briard.
Right: Bernese Mountain Dog.
Below right: Bichon Frisé puppy.

The color is black with smaller tan markings on the foreface and legs, a white blaze on the head, and a white 'shirt front.' The height at the shoulder is 25 to 28 inches for dogs, 23 to 26 inches for bitches.

Bichon Frisé *France*

The name Bichon (literally lap dog) has often been used to describe a family of small, usually white dogs to which the Belgian Bichon, the Maltese, the Teneriffe Dog, and the French Bichon à Poil Frisé belong. In recent years the latter – as the Bichon Frisé – has been introduced into the United States where it has become especially popular, although the breed has yet to be recognized by the American Kennel Club.

It is not unlike the Maltese but its curly, silky hair is more profuse, especially on the head. The color of the Bichon Frisé is white or white with apricot or dark gray patches on the ears and body. The height at the shoulder should be between 8 and 12 inches.

Under this heading the Bichon Havanais deserves a passing mention. As its name implies this breed has Cuban connections, but while it has existed in Cuba for several hundred years its ancestors must have come from Italy or France. In build the Bichon Havanais is similar to the Maltese and the Bichon Frisé, having a broad skull, dark eyes, and dropped ears folded forward. The coat is long and silky, ranging in color from white and fawn to tobacco brown.

Bichon Petit Chien Lion, see **Lion dogs**

Black and Tan Coonhound, see
American Coonhound

Black and Tan Miniature *Britain*
This is one of the names by which the Toy
Manchester Terrier is known. See *English
Toy Terrier* (Black and Tan).

Blenheim Spaniel, see **Cavalier King
Charles Spaniel**

Bloodhound *Britain*
The Bloodhound is now regarded as a pure
British breed since it has been mostly used
and appreciated by Britain for centuries,
but its original forebears were French.
Nowadays it is kept primarily as a wrinkled
and good-humored pet but, because of its
sensitive nose and ability to follow a trail,
it is sometimes used as a tracker dog.

The Bloodhound is a large, powerful
animal with a dignified expression. Its
skin is loose and baggy, the head long and
narrow with long, thin, and very soft,
pendulous ears. The coat is short and
usually black and/or tan. The average
height at the shoulder for dogs is 26 inches,
24 inches for bitches. The weight should be
at least 90 pounds and 80 pounds each.

Border Collie *Britain*
The Border Collie is not officially recognized as a breed. Nevertheless, it deserves
a mention in this catalog of dogs if only
because it is highly rated as a sheepdog,
even outside Britain.

The Border Collie comes from the
Border country between England and
Scotland. It resembles a small and very
much less refined version of the Rough
Collie; the head is broader and coarser,
the ears not as elegantly set and carried, and
the coat is not as profuse.

The color is usually black with white
markings, and the height at the shoulder
is about 18 to 20 inches.

Border Terrier *Britain*
Like the Border Collie, the tough little
Border Terrier originated in the Cheviot
Hills bordering on Scotland. It was bred
and developed as a working terrier to
hunt and destroy the foxes which preyed
on the sheep in that region. Nowadays,
however, most Border Terriers are kept as
suburban pets, a role for which they are
ideally suited because they are small,
clean, adaptable, loyal, and gentle with
children.

The Border Terrier is an active and
hardy little dog with a dense and somewhat harsh coat. The head is shaped like
that of an otter, the eyes dark, the ears
small. Color varies – red, sandy, sandy and
tan, or blue and tan. The weight for dogs
varies between 13 and $15\frac{1}{2}$ pounds, bitches
between $11\frac{1}{2}$ and 14 pounds. The height at
the shoulder is 11 to 14 inches.

Above right: Border Collie.
Right: Border Terrier.
Below: Bloodhounds.

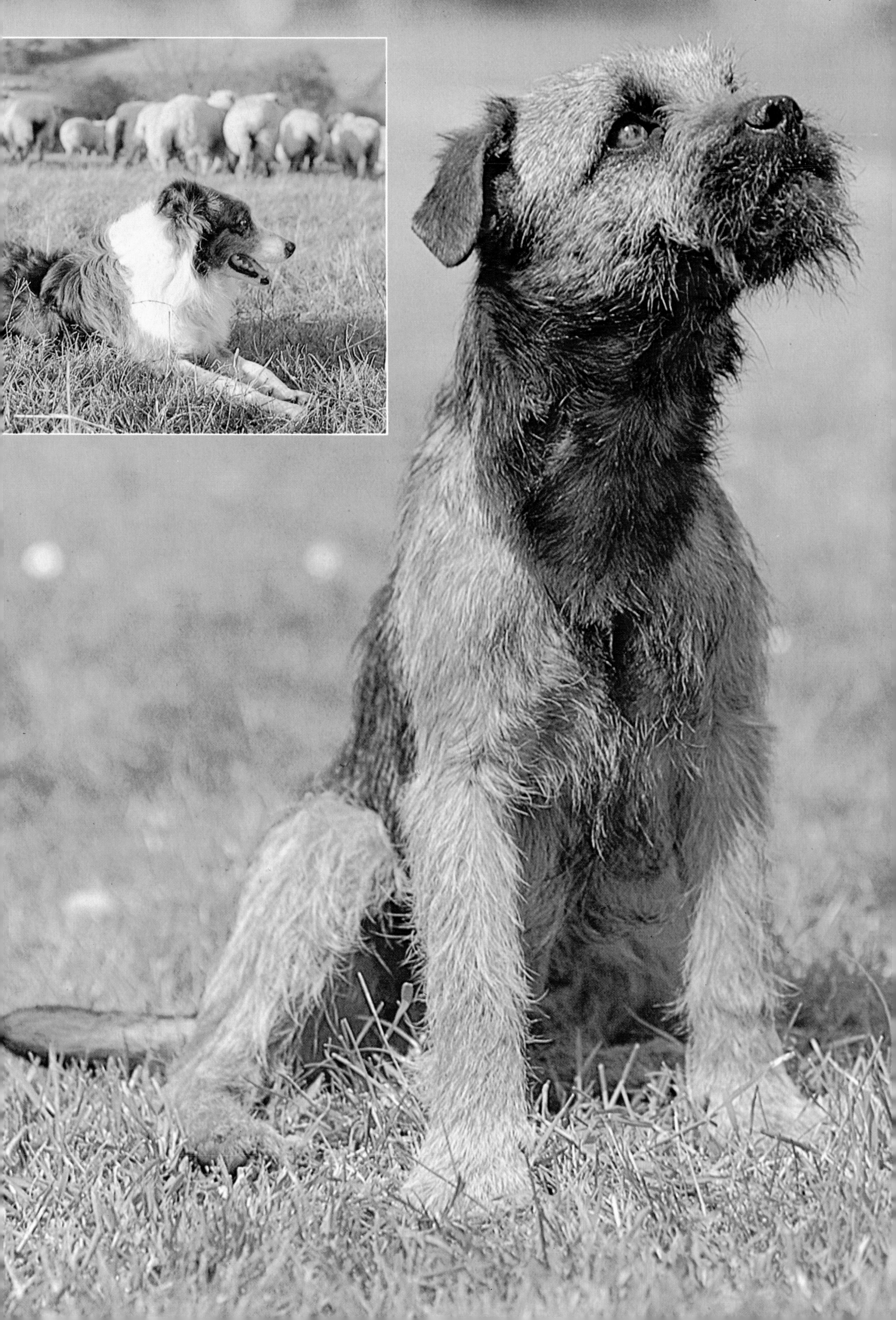

Borzoi *USSR*

The Borzoi is one of the traditional beauties of the canine world. It came to the West from the USSR and, until comparatively recently, it was known as the Russian Wolfhound. Before the Revolution the aristocracy of the Russian Imperial Court kept teams of Borzois, and the Czar himself maintained a kennel of several hundred for the traditional sport of hunting the wolf. Despite this background, the Borzoi has a friendly temperament. It is a graceful dog with great muscular power and speed; the head is of classical mold, long, lean, and narrow with almond-shaped eyes. The body is rather narrow but with great depth of brisket, the back rising in a graceful arch and covered in a long, silky, flat, or curly coat. The long, elegant tail has profuse and soft feathering.

The Czar reputedly preferred light-colored dogs, but all colors are acceptable. The height at the shoulder for dogs is from 29 inches, bitches from 27 inches.

Boston Terrier *USA*

The jaunty little Boston Terrier is one of the breeds recommended as a pet, especially for families with children or novice dog owners; few breeds are so easy to manage and such pleasant companions. Yet the Boston Terrier descends from dogs which could not have been more unsuitable for family life. During the nineteenth century, dogfights, with lively betting and a great deal of money at stake, were a national sport in Britain and the USA. Originally, Bulldogs and terriers were used but, when someone hit on the idea of combining the strength of the Bulldog with the tenacity of the terrier, the forerunner of the Boston Terrier breed was born.

Since then American and British breeders have reduced its size and made it a delightful and affectionate companion without extinguishing the terrier spark. It has spread and gained popularity nearly all over the world. The Boston Terrier is easy to train and makes a good family companion.

Although the Boston Terrier is one of the smaller breeds, it does not give the impression of being a toy dog; its compact body and stylish deportment demonstrate that it is determined, strong, and active.

Brindle and white is the most desirable color, but black and white is acceptable; any other color is unacceptable. The distribution of the white markings is usually considered of great importance: ideally there is a white blaze over the head, white muzzle, neck, chest, forelegs, and hind legs below the hocks. The height at the shoulder should not exceed 16 inches.

Above: Borzoi.
Right: Boston Terrier.

Bouledogue Français *France*

The French Bulldog, the 'Frenchie' as it is known in pet circles, is best described as a miniature version of the British Bulldog. The breed is descended from Bulldogs exported to France from Britain and subsequently interbred with various Continental toy breeds. In nineteenth-century Paris, the French Bulldog became a sign of fashion and was bred fairly extensively, in spite of the fact that British breeders regarded it as a crossbreed. Nowadays many of the best animals are produced by British breeders, which is proof – if any were needed – of the 'Frenchie's' winning ways.

The French Bulldog is compactly built, well boned, and thick set. Despite its slightly pugnacious expression, it is a friendly dog. The body is higher at the loins than at the shoulder, but the front legs should not be crooked. The coat is smooth and lustrous.

The color is brindle, white, pied, or fawn. In Britain the ideal weight is 28 pounds for dogs, 24 pounds for bitches. The American Kennel Club has two classes: lightweights under 22 pounds, and heavyweights over 22 pounds but under a maximum of 28 pounds.

Bouvier de Flanders *Belgium*

A Bouvier always attracts attention – it is rare, it is of considerable size, and its appearance is distinguished. It is not unlike the Giant Schnauzer, but is even heavier and bigger boned. Like the Groenendael and the Tervueren, the Bouvier comes from Belgium where it was used for herding cattle. Gradually the type produced in Flanders was bred. Not surprisingly the breed was almost destroyed in World War I and there were very few Bouviers left in Belgium after World War II.

The Bouvier is robust and thick set but gives a general impression of style and presence. The coat is double with a thick, soft undercoat and a harsh top coat, particularly abundant on the head where it forms moustaches, chin whiskers, and eyebrows which, according to the breed standard, gives the dog an unkempt look.

The color may vary from pale fawn to dark gray, sometimes black and red particolor. The height at the shoulder is about 26 inches and weight 66 pounds.

Right: French Bulldog.
Far right: Bouvier de Flanders.

Boxer *Germany*

The Boxer is a popular pet. Usually out-classed by the German Shepherd as a working dog, it is friendly, fond of children, and much more playful than its somewhat 'puzzled' expression would suggest.

It has, of course, a great deal in common with the Bulldog. In ancient Greece bull breeds were used as fighting dogs, but it was not until the Middle Ages that they were developed into dogs used for hunting larger game and eventually as sheepdogs. Toward the end of the nineteenth century, the Boxer evolved into a type clearly distinguishable from a Bulldog. The derivation of the name Boxer is uncertain, but it is unlikely that it has anything to do with 'the noble art.'

The Boxer is muscular and clean cut. The shape of the head is its most important characteristic; the muzzle should be well developed, broad and square with a slightly underhung lower jaw. The coat should be short and shiny.

The color is brindle, red, or pied with a dark mask round the eyes and muzzle. Dogs stand 22 to 25 inches at the shoulder, bitches 21 to 23 inches.

Braque d'Auvergne *France*

Braque (or brack) is a term used to describe some breeds of hunting dogs – hounds, setters, or pointers. The French breeds belonging to the braque group are numerous and similar in type, not only to other French varieties but to foreign breeds as well. The Braque d'Auvergne, for example, strongly resembles both the English Pointer and the German Short-haired Pointer.

Opinions differ regarding its origin. Some people consider that it is descended from the old French Braque which later interbred with more recent breeds; others believe that it was brought to France from Malta by Napoleon's returning troops.

The Braque d'Auvergne is powerful, imposing, and elegant. The eyes are nut brown with a bold expression, the ears pendulous, long, and smooth as satin. The tail is carried level with the back and is usually docked to 6 to 8 inches. The coat is short, lustrous, and weather resistant.

The most desirable color is white with bluish-black spots of varying size and distribution. The head, however, is always self-colored (a single, whole color except for shadings). The ideal height at the shoulder for dogs is 23 to 25 inches, 22 to 24 inches for bitches.

Braque Français *France*

The original French Braque is believed to be one of the oldest breeds of hound still

extant. Over the years it has contributed to the development of not only many native breeds, but also of several foreign ones, the Pointer, for example, is believed to descend from the French Braque, although the British considerably changed and improved it.

The French Braque is a powerful dog without appearing too heavy. The nose is chestnut brown, as are the eyes, though these may also be dark amber with a grave, affectionate expression. The loins are slightly arched and the tail, which is usually docked short, is carried in line with the back. Long tails are, however, acceptable. The coat is very short and close, and softer on the head and ears than on the body.

The color is white with chestnut-colored patches and lighter or darker shadings. The height at the shoulder may vary between 22 and 26 inches.

Braque Saint-Germain *France*

The French Braque Saint-Germain is thought to have originated as the result of a cross of an English Pointer with a French Braque early in the nineteenth century.

Although the Braque Saint-Germain resembles the Pointer, it is not as muscular or as heavily boned. The head is less distinctive than the Pointer's, the nose flesh colored and the eyes amber. The tail is carried, like the Pointer's, in line with the back and is not docked. The coat is short but fairly coarse.

The color is white with bright orange markings. Dogs stand 20 to 25 inches at the shoulder, bitches 21 to 23 inches.

Above: Braque d'Auvergne.
Right: Boxer and Braque St Germain (above far right).

Brazilian Tracker (Rastreador Brasileiro) *Brazil*

As its name suggests this breed originated in Brazil where it is used by hunters to track the South American jaguar. It was created by crossbreeding a variety of breeds, primarily American Foxhounds and Coonhounds and looks rather like a Coonhound, with a large, deep chest, and long tail. The hair is short and rough, the eyes yellow, the head flat and round.

Briard, see **Berger de la Brie**

Briquet Griffon Vendéen, *France*

This is a smaller variety of the Grand Griffon Vendéen. The height at the shoulder is between 20 and 22 inches for dogs, and 19 and 21 inches for bitches.

Brittany Spaniel, *see* **Epagneul Breton**

Bulldog *Britain*

The Bulldog is essentially a British breed; indeed, in a popular nineteenth century song Britishers were described as 'boys of the Bulldog breed' due to their pugnacity.

In the fourteenth century, Bulldogs were used in the ancient sport of bullbaiting. The dogs were trained to seize the bull by the nose and not let go until the bull fell. In the nineteenth century, when bull-baiting was declared illegal, the Bulldogs were in danger of becoming extinct. But thanks to a few dedicated breeders the temperament improved and the Bulldog was to become part of the old John Bull image as the British national breed.

The Bulldog is thick set and broad, slightly higher at the loins than at the shoulders. The head is large with a short muzzle and a turned-up lower jaw protruding considerably in front of the upper jaw. It has dark eyes and small 'rose ears.' The tail is short, the coat close and smooth.

Color varies considerably, mostly in combination with white, and most varieties are acceptable. Weight is usually around 55 pounds; the breed standard does not specify height.

Bullmastiff *Britain*

Outside Britain the heavy and powerful Bullmastiff is comparatively rare. The breed is believed to have resulted from crossbreeding Bulldogs with Mastiffs. In the latter part of the nineteenth century poaching was rife and gamekeepers needed agile, aggressive dogs capable of attacking intruders when ordered to do so, throwing them down, and holding until ordered to release – but never savaging or mauling. This specification was met when the ferocious and determined Bulldog was crossed with the formidable but less aggressive Mastiff.

The Bullmastiff is massive and heavily built without appearing clumsy. The head is large and square with a short muzzle and dark eyes. The coat is short and close.

The color is brindle, fawn, or red with a dark mask round the eyes and on the muzzle. The height at the shoulder for dogs is 25 to 27 inches, 24 to 26 inches for bitches. The weight is 90 to 130 pounds.

Right and below: Bulldog.
Bottom: Bullmastiff.

Bull Terrier *Britain*

When bullbaiting became illegal in Britain, the British turned to dogfighting, and for this a type of dog was needed which was lithe and quick but just as strong and vicious as before. So Bulldogs were crossed with terriers and the result was a 'bull and terrier dog.' Other crosses were then made which gave the Bull Terrier its characteristic conformation and its more controllable temper.

It is strong and muscular without appearing clumsy. The head is a main feature; it is distinctly egg shaped. The coat is short and glossy. The color is white, brindle, or colored with white markings. There are neither weight nor height limits laid down in the breed standard, but the height at the shoulder is usually about 16 inches.

The Miniature Bull Terrier is what its name implies – a small-size Bull Terrier, with a height of not more than 14 inches and weighing not more than 20 pounds. As a breed it is recognized in comparatively few countries outside Britain.

Butterfly Dog, see Papillon

Cairn Terrier *Britain*

In Britain the lively little Cairn Terrier is a very popular pet and companion. It comes from Inverness in Scotland, and in its early days the breed had much in common with the Skye Terrier. First known as the Short-haired Terrier and then as the West Highland Terrier, it was accepted in 1910 by the Kennel Club as the Cairn Terrier. (The word 'cairn,' a pile of stones, comes from the Gaelic word for 'a heap'; it is therefore an appropriate name for a Scot-

tish breed eager to 'go to ground.')

The Cairn Terrier is an active and hardy little dog with a shaggy coat, a bold bearing, and a somewhat fox-like expression.

The color varies from sandy to nearly black. Darker shadings on ears and muzzle are very typical. The height at the shoulder is about 10 inches, the weight about 14 pounds.

Canaan Dog *Israel*

Outside Israel, where it has been bred as a sheepdog, the Canaan Dog is a rarity (with the possible exception of the United States, where in recent years it has become quite fashionable). The Canaan Dog is of the spitz type and it has a tendency to roam and fight. If well treated it can become a very affectionate pet and an excellent guard dog.

The Canaan Dog has erect ears, but drop ears are also acceptable. The eyes are very dark; lack of pigmentation on the nose is normal for particolored dogs, and acceptable also for dogs of other colors. When the dog is alert, the tail is carried in an arch over the back and is heavily plumed. The coat is of medium length, straight, and coarse. Long-coated and short-coated dogs are acceptable but undesirable.

The color ranges from sandy to reddish brown, white, or black. Common and acceptable varieties are particolor, piebald, or Boston markings. The height at the shoulder varies between 20 and 24 inches.

Below: Cairn Terrier.
Left: Bull Terrier.
Far left: Miniature Bull Terrier.

Cavalier King Charles Spaniel *Britain*

The friendly, affectionate little Cavalier King Charles Spaniel is often confused with its close relative and forerunner, the King Charles Spaniel. Both breeds take their name from King Charles II, who kept large numbers of toy spaniels and was devoted to them. At that time King Charles Spaniels looked rather like diminutive Cockers. However, their appearance started to change around the middle of the nineteenth century at a time when everything oriental was fashionable. Crossed with short-nosed toy breeds imported from China and Japan, the King Charles became smaller in size, shorter in the muzzle and nose, and more rounded in the skull.

The next development came about 1920 when a Mr Eldridge, an American living on Long Island, decided that the King Charles Spaniels were no longer like the little spaniels which adorn canvases and tapestries painted by the great masters of the sixteenth and seventeenth centuries. So Eldridge offered cash prizes at Cruft's Dog Show for 'Blenheim Spaniels of the old type – with long faces, flat skulls, no inclination to be domed, no stop, and a beauty spot in the center of the forehead.' The result was the Cavalier King Charles breed which rapidly gained popularity, although it was not recognized officially as a breed until 1944. In 1960 the popularity of Cavaliers was further boosted when Princess Margaret acquired one; they are now among the 20 most popular breeds.

In conformation, the Cavalier resembles an old hunting spaniel in miniature; it is active, graceful, spirited, and sturdily built.

There are four color varieties: *black and tan* (pure black with small brown markings), *Blenheim* (white with chestnut-red markings and a white blaze on the forehead), *tricolor* (black and white with small tan markings), and *ruby* (a whole-colored rich red). The breed standard does not specify height at the shoulder. The weight is 10 to 18 pounds.

Chesapeake Bay Retriever *USA*

The Chesapeake Bay Retriever is the American 'water dog.' It is strikingly similar in build to the British Labrador Retriever and tradition has it that the breed is descended from two Newfoundland puppies rescued from an English brig which was wrecked off the coast of Maryland. But, as distinct from other related breeds, the Chesapeake Bay Retriever has pure yellow eyes and a very special coat: slightly wavy on the back and very short, tough, and thick on the body in order to withstand cold and wet when working in icy waters. The coat should feel decidedly oily to the touch and should be so water-resistant that once the dog has come ashore and given itself a shake, it should feel hardly damp! The color is also considered very important; in order that the dog should merge with its background as far as possible, the breed standard lays down a 'dead grass' color ranging from dark brown to faded tan – preferably without small white markings on chest and feet. Dogs stand 23 to 26 inches at the shoulder, bitches 21 to 24 inches.

Right: Chesapeake Bay Retriever.
Below: Black and tan Cavalier King Charles Spaniel.

84

Chihuahua *Mexico*

There are two breeds of the world's smallest dog, which is named after the Mexican state and city of Chihuahua: the Long-coat Chihuahua and the Smooth-coat Chihuahua. Many of the early American breeders believed that the Long-coat was the original Chihuahua, but it was the Smooth-coat that first caught the public's fancy. In effect, the Long-coat is identical to the Smooth-coat except for its long and soft-textured coat, which is either flat or slightly wavy and particularly abundant on ears, neck, and tail.

All colors or mixture of colors are acceptable in both varieties of Chihuahua, which is yet another point of difference between the Long-coat and the Papillon. The Long-coat, however, may be slightly larger than its smooth-coated cousin and can weigh up to about 8 pounds.

The Smooth-coat Chihuahua may be the true Mexican breed, and the Long-coat a mixture of Smooth-coat and toy breeds. Whether or not this is true, and despite their being so small, both Long-coat and Smooth-coat Chihuahuas have tremendous personalities.

The Smooth-coat Chihuahua is a neat, alert little dog with a saucy expression. The skull is 'apple domed,' the eyes round and dark or matching the color of the coat. Ruby eyes are considered very desirable.

Any color or mixture of colors is accept-able. The weight should be up to 6 pounds, preferably 2 to 4 pounds. The breed standard does not specify height.

Chinese Crested Dog, see Hairless dogs

Chow Chow *China*

The Chow Chow has a long and interesting history. Originally it came from China where, up to about 1000 BC, it was used as a temple dog to frighten off evil spirits. For this purpose Chows with a frowning and threatening expression were preferred. The breed came to Europe in the eighteenth century and has since become very popular as a companion and pet.

According to breed standard, the Chow is 'leonine [like a lion] with a dignified bearing and aloof expression.' It is active and well balanced but with a stilted gait. The head is large and broad with small, slightly rounded erect ears and has a bluish-black tongue. The body is short and level, the legs well boned and straight. The tail, set high, is carried well over the back.

There is a smooth-coated variety, but this is very rare. Normally the Chow has a thick, straight coat, particularly abundant round the neck (the 'lion's mane'). The color is black, red, fawn, cream, blue, or white, never particolored. The height at the shoulder is at least 18 inches.

Right: Long-coat and Smooth-coat (inset) Chihuahua.
Below: Chow Chow blue.

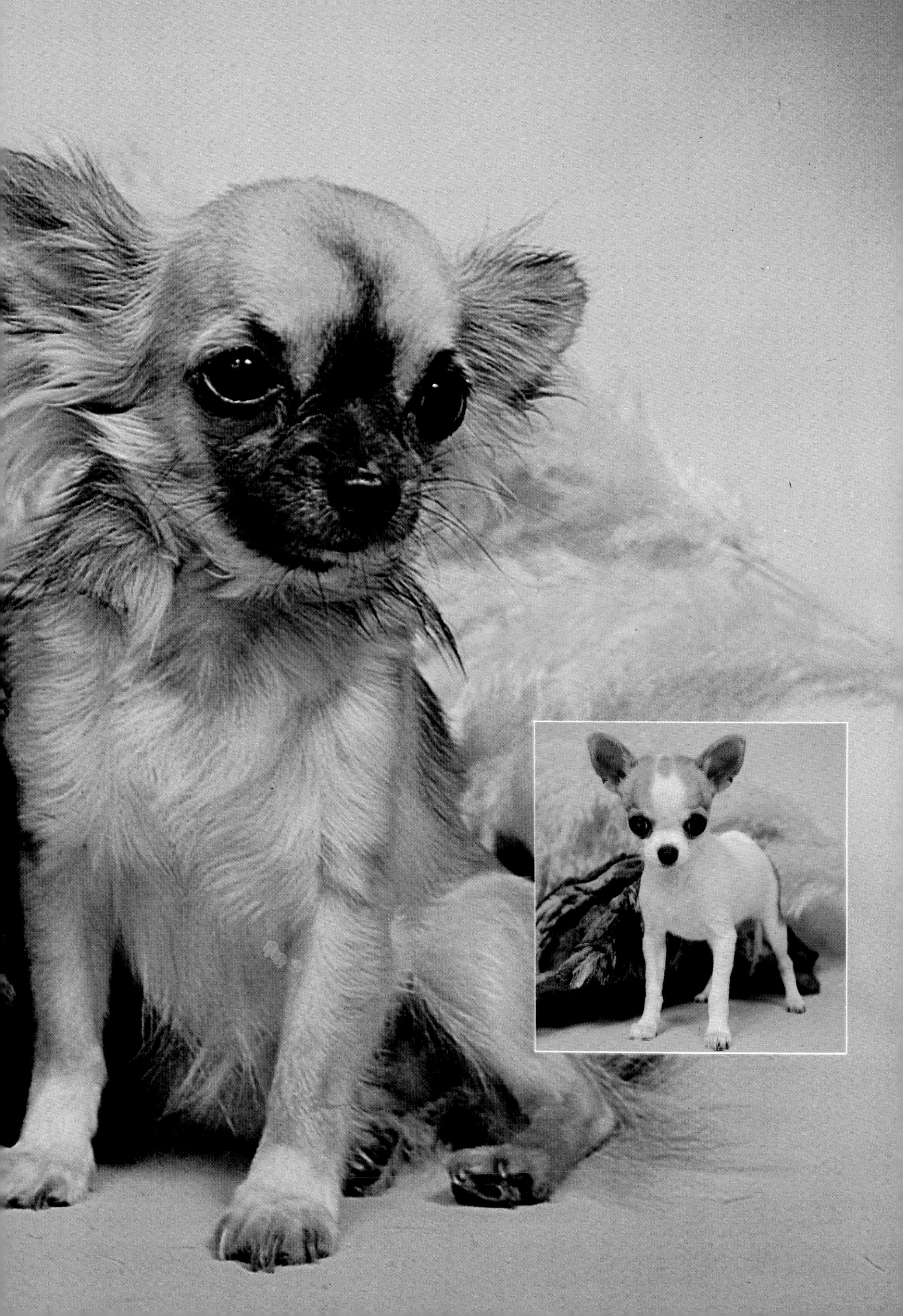

Clumber Spaniel *Britain*

The Clumber Spaniel, which has been advertised as the breed for the individual, is rare enough in its home country and it is even more of a rarity outside Britain. At one time they were thought to be descended from Alpine Spaniels and thus related to St Bernards, and they were also said to have reached England originally as a gift from the Duc de Noailles to the Duke of Newcastle at Clumber Park in 1875. Both stories are unlikely. It is more probable that these dogs were bred at Clumber from the dogs which were there at that time. In any event, the Clumber breed had its heyday toward the end of the nineteenth century when it was used as a gundog; King Edward VII was particularly fond of them and King George V used them exclusively on the Sandringham estate.

According to the breed standard, the Clumber is a heavy and massive dog with a thoughtful expression. As a gundog breed it also needs to be active. The head is large and square with a broad skull and pronounced occiput (lower back part of the skull). The muzzle is heavy and deep with a flesh-colored nose, the eyes are dark and the ears large and vine-leaf shaped. The body is long and heavy and the legs short, very well boned, and strong. The tail is short, the coat close, silky, and straight. The legs, tail, and belly (but not the ears) are well feathered.

The color is white with smaller lemon markings. Weight varies from 45 to 70 pounds.

Clydesdale Terrier *Britain*

The Clydesdale Terrier – also sometimes known as a Paisley Terrier – was a forerunner of the Skye Terrier. Dissension among breeders caused it to fall out of favor and by the mid-1930s the breed was no longer recognized and had ceased to be exhibited at dog shows. According to the records Clydesdales were bred in and around Glasgow (which is in the Clyde River Valley, and of which Paisley is a suburb), and it was said originally to have been the result of crosses of a Dandie Dinmont, a Poodle, and a Yorkshire Terrier.

Cocker Spaniel *Britain*

It is not certain how the Cocker acquired its name. Either it was because it was used to spring or 'cock' the game for the gun, or, more likely, because of its special aptitude when used to start woodcock. The Cocker Spaniel, known in some countries as the English Cocker Spaniel, is one of the most popular breeds in the world. It deserves to be so, for it is a friendly little dog with a cheerful and affectionate temperament – a dog that can charm the hardest heart. It is, in fact, a gundog and, although it is more often kept as a pet, it usually manages to find some suitable outlet for its boundless energy. Although the spaniel type has been known for centuries in Britain, the Cocker was not recognized as a breed until just before the turn of the twentieth century. It did not gain its present vast popularity until after World War II.

The Cocker Spaniel is an active little sporting dog with a friendly, trusting disposition. The head is cleanly chiselled with flat cheeks and a marked stop. The eyes are full and of a color harmonizing with the coat. The ears are low-set, long, and supple. The body is compact and deep, the legs well boned with round feet. The tail is docked fairly short, is carried low, and is incessantly active. The coat is smooth and silky with long, soft feathering on the ears, chest, and on the back of the legs.

The color may vary from solid colors to particolors or roans (white speckled with black, lemon, orange, or liver). The ideal height at the shoulder is about 16 inches.

Corgi, see **Welsh Corgi**

Curly-coated Retriever *Britain*

The coat of the Curly-coated Retriever distinguishes it from other retriever breeds and indicates its Irish Water Spaniel and Poodle ancestry. In addition to this lineage it is also descended from the same type of Old English hunting spaniel and imported Canadian dogs as the Golden and Labrador Retrievers. As an established breed it is, however, one of the oldest within the group.

The Curly-coated Retriever is a strong, smart, upstanding dog. It is also intelligent and active with great stamina. The head is powerful with a moderately flat skull, the eyes are black or brown and rather large, but not too prominent. The ears are small, lying close to the head. The neck, body, and legs are strong and muscular. The tail is moderately short and is carried fairly straight. The coat is the main characteristic of the breed: it is a mass of small, crisp curls all over, including the ears and tail but excluding the muzzle. The close-fitting coat is impervious to water.

The color is black or liver. The height at the shoulder is about 25 to 27 inches.

Top right: Cocker Spaniel.
Above right: Clumber Spaniel.
Right: Curly-coated Retriever.

Smooth-haired Dachshund (above). Wire-haired Dachshund (below right) and with a Long-haired variety (right).

Dachsbracke and Westfälische Dachsbracke *Germany*

The Dachsbracke is one of the less common breeds. It looks very much like a heavier, longer-legged, and coarser version of the Smooth Dachshund. In Germany it is used for tracking by scent. There are several colors: black and tan markings; different shades of tan; or white with tan markings. The height at the shoulder is 13 to 17 inches.

The Westfälische Dachsbracke is a smaller variety colored generally reddish-fawn with white markings, although black and chocolate brown are also common. Height at the shoulder is 12 to 14 inches.

Dachshund *Germany*

The Dachshund (which means in German 'Badger dog') is one of the most popular breeds in Europe and it has evolved into six varieties; there are now standard and miniature sizes in Long-haired, Smooth-haired, and Wire-haired Dachshunds.

As its name implies, the Dachshund is an 'earth dog,' a terrier. But when Dachshunds were first introduced into England, 'hund' was translated as 'hound' and the Dachshund was considered to be in the hound group – where he has remained for over a century. (Dachshunds became popular in England because of Queen Victoria's Dashy and the other Dachshunds brought from Germany by Prince Albert.)

Short-legged terriers, which were the ancestors of the modern Dachshund, existed in Germany over a thousand years ago. Naturally the breed has changed over the centuries. In the early days it was used for hunting underground, and more recently for tracking game and driving it to the guns. Now Dachshunds are kept mainly as pets.

There has been considerable argument as to how the division into different sizes and coat textures came about. Dachshunds of all types, however, evolved through mutations several hundred years ago, but while the smooth-haired and long-haired types quickly gained popularity, the wire-haired variety was gradually pushed into the background and for a time disappeared. It was not until the end of the nineteenth century that attempts were made to revive the wire-haired, and Schnauzers and Dandie Dinmont Terriers were used, among others, as outcrosses. The methods used were successful and the wire-haireds of today are of as high a quality as the other coat varieties.

There are two smaller versions of the Dachshund: the Miniature Dachshund and an even smaller type known in some countries as the 'Rabbit' Dachshund, with measurements around the girth not exceeding 14 inches and 12 inches respectively. These miniatures evolved in Germany at the turn of this century, mainly through crosses between the smallest of the standard varieties, though other small breeds were also used. The Miniatures and 'Rabbit' Dachshunds can be either wire-haired, smooth-haired, or long-haired.

The Dachshund is active, bold, and alert. It is short-legged with a long body and proud carriage. The head is long and well chiselled and tapers gradually to the nose. The eyes are almond-shaped and should not be lighter than chestnut brown. The ears are rounded and lie close to the cheek. The neck is long and moderately arched, the back long and slightly curved over the loin, the legs short, straight, and well boned.

The color varies from black and tan to red, chocolate, brindle, and dapple. A standard Dachshund of average size should weigh not more than 20 pounds.

Dalmatian *Yugoslavia*

The name Dalmatian implies that this breed hails from Dalmatia on the Adriatic coast, and Yugoslavia is taken to be its official native country. But there is no real proof to indicate that this is so and various theories have been put forward that the spotted dog originated in countries as diverse as Denmark, Spain, Egypt, and India. Nowadays, because there is some evidence of Dalmatians accompanying gypsies from the Far East during the Middle Ages, India is favored as the most likely country of origin. Today the Dalmatian could almost be classed as a British breed, for it has been very popular in Britain since the eighteenth century when upper-class Englishmen kept it as a decorative carriage dog, running between the high carriage wheels.

The Dalmatian is an agile, symmetrical, and muscular dog with active movement. Eye color depends on the markings and may even be yellow in liver-spotted dogs.

Color and markings are its most prominent characteristics. The ideal Dalmatian is evenly marked all over with small, round, black or liver spots. The height at the shoulder is 20 inches.

Dandie Dinmont *Britain*

The Dandie Dinmont Terrier is an unusual breed and in many parts of the world it is regarded as a canine curiosity. However, in Britain it has had a fairly large following since it featured in Sir Walter Scott's novels at the beginning of the nineteenth century. (Scott created a character called Dandie Dinmont, a Border farmer who kept somewhat scruffy terriers, and people who owned similar dogs referred to them as 'Dandie Dinmont Terriers.')

Originally the Dandie Dinmont was a wire-haired hunting terrier in the Cheviot Hills but, after its sudden climb to popularity, it was bred to fit more easily into drawing-room life and developed its present quaint looks.

It is a long-bodied, short-legged dog with a large head profusely covered with soft silky hair. The body is low at the shoulders with an arch over the loins and a slight drop from the loin toward the root of the tail. The tail is moderately long and carried in line with the back or slightly above it; the coat is a mixture of soft and fairly hard hair.

The color ranges from a dark bluish-black to a pale fawn. The height at the shoulder is 8 to 11 inches and the ideal weight is about 18 pounds.

Above right: Dandie Dinmont.
Right: Dalmatian.

Deerhound *Scotland*

The Scottish Deerhound is another breed made famous by Sir Walter Scott. (The artist Landseer, who painted some remarkable pictures of Deerhounds, and Queen Victoria were also very fond of the breed.) It is believed that the ancestors of today's Deerhounds accompanied Phoenician traders to Britain, where eventually they became established in the Scottish Highlands. For a long time the Deerhound and the Irish Wolfhound were considered varieties of the same type of dog and the two breeds could not be properly distinguished until the nineteenth century. Today, however, they are easy to tell apart; even though the Deerhound may often be as tall as the Wolfhound, it is always considerably lighter and more graceful in build and possesses the distinct characteristics of the sighthound. The Deerhound can perhaps more accurately be described as a wire-haired Greyhound. In temperament it is usually docile and friendly.

It is built on racy lines with a wiry, shaggy, blue-gray coat, dark eyes, small, thin, black ears, and a tail which almost reaches the ground. The height at the shoulder is at least 30 inches for dogs and at least 28 inches for bitches. The weight is 85 to 105 pounds and 65 to 80 pounds respectively.

Dingo *Australia*

The Dingo, or Warrigal, is the only true wild dog and it is native to Australia. A very long time ago it was probably a domestic dog but for unknown reasons it returned to the wild state. However, the same mortal enmity that is shown by the wolf to the domestic dog does not exist between the Dingo and his domestic counterpart, and in Australia there has been considerable interbreeding between the two breeds.

In size the Dingo is between the wolf and the jackal, with many being about 22 inches tall at the shoulder. It is generally yellowish-red to brown in color but many have patches of white on the belly, the tail, and the feet. Dingoes hunt singly or in pairs, rarely in packs.

Dobermann Pinscher *Germany*

The Dobermann Pinscher ('Pinscher' means terrier and the breed is known simply as the Dobermann in the United States and Canada) is named after the German dog catcher Dobermann, who at the turn of the twentieth century used some of his stray dogs to breed as mean and as vicious a dog as possible. Conformation was of secondary importance, but as far as temperament was concerned he succeeded beyond expectation. After Dobermann's time, the breed was crossed with, among others, Manchester Terriers and Greyhounds and has since improved in conformation and become more manageable in temperament.

Today's Dobermann is a clean-cut, powerful, and elegant dog. Indeed it is said that a first-class Dobermann is one of the most handsome creatures of the canine world. Its color is black or liver brown with tan markings. Dogs stand about 26 inches at the shoulder, bitches about 25 inches. The weight is about 55 pounds.

Left: Deerhound
Above right: Dingo.
Right: Dobermann Pinscher.

Dogue de Bordeaux *France*

The Dogue de Bordeaux is relatively rare, even in France, and is practically never seen outside it. It closely resembles the English Bullmastiff, for which it is often mistaken. Considered to be rather sulky and moody, it is a heavy, thickset dog with a large, broad head. The nose is usually dark but may be lighter in dogs with a tan mask. The eyes are large and set wide apart. The tail is usually carried low. The coat is smooth and short.

Mahogany, golden, or gray are the most desirable colors. The height at the shoulder varies from 23 to 26 inches, with bitches proportionally smaller. The weight may be up to about 100 pounds.

Dunkerstövare *Norway*

Outside its home country, the Norwegian Dunkerstövare is a comparatively rare breed. It is a powerful dog with great stamina. The head is fairly long with a marked stop, a straight foreface, and usually dark eyes; light-color eyes are, however, acceptable in piebald varieties. The ears are carried close to the head. The tail, which should be as straight as possible, reaches the hock. The coat is coarse, thick, and close.

The color is black or piebald with white, brown, or fawn markings. The height at the shoulder is 18 to 23 inches.

Eastern Greyhound

The term Eastern Greyhound describes a group of loosely related dogs, including the Arab Greyhound (generally known as the Saluki), Persian and Afghan Greyhounds which together became Afghan Hounds, and Rampur, Banjara, and Mahratta Greyhounds – all Saluki-type dogs from India.

Elkhound, see Norwegian Elkhound

English Coonhound *USA*

Strictly speaking, the name English Coonhound is inaccurate since the breed was evolved in the USA. However, to distinguish this variety, its British origin was seized upon. There is Foxhound blood in its pedigree, even though this has become diluted through interbreeding. Like its American counterpart the English Coonhound is used for hunting in some regions – both raccoon and other small game.

In comparison with the Black and Tan Coonhound, the English variety is relatively lightly built and lacks the stamp of Bloodhound. The height at the shoulder is about 26 inches.

Far left: Norwegian Elkhound.
Left: Dogue de Bordeaux.

English Foxhound *Britain*

Although the English Foxhound is a thoroughbred, and one of the best known, most publicized, frequently painted and photographed of any of the English dogs, it rarely appears at recognized dog shows in Britain. The reason for this is reputed to be the British determination to preserve the Foxhound as a pure working breed; Foxhounds exported from Britain in recent years have, however, been shown in some countries.

Looks are of secondary importance to working abilities and breed type varies a great deal. The color is usually tan with a black saddle, and white markings on the foreface, chest, belly, legs, and tail, or white with black, tan, or lemon markings. The height at the shoulder is about 24 inches.

The main difference between the American Foxhound and its English ancestor breed is size. The American dog is generally a bigger, long-legged dog with a strong body. Otherwise there is little to distinguish the two breeds, but in the United States the American Foxhound has become a comparatively popular show dog.

English Setter *Britain*

Most people would concede that the English Setter, with his graceful lines, limpid eyes, and the friendly nature symbolized by his gently waving tail, is one of the most attractive of all breeds of dog. It originated from English hunting spaniels and, as a result of intensive selective breeding, was firmly established by the middle of the nineteenth century, when for some time it was the leading breed both at shows and in the field. In type it has remained about the same over the past 300 years, but more recently a heavier type has been evolved for show in Britain.

The English Setter has an appearance of elegance, strength, and speed. The head is long with a fairly lean skull and a marked stop, a straight, deep muzzle, and expressive, dark eyes. The back slopes toward the scimitar-shaped tail which tapers off toward the tip. The long and glossy coat is particularly long on the ears, chest, tail, and on the back of the legs.

In color, white predominates with markings in black, lemon, or liver; sometimes tricolor (black, white, and tan). The height at the shoulder is about 25 inches.

Above: A pack of English Foxhounds.

Right: English Setter and English Setter puppy.

English Springer Spaniel *Britain*

There are eight different varieties of spaniel. Of these the Cockers are the most popular, the Field the most rare, the Irish Water Spaniel the tallest, and the Clumber the heaviest. The English Springer is the most robust of the varieties and it is credited with a more even temperament.

Setters and spaniels are descended from the same type of gundog but, while setters became established as a type fairly quickly, weight was the only deciding factor in distinguishing Cockers from Springers up to the end of the nineteenth century.

The English Springer Spaniel is a medium-sized, strong, and active dog. The color of the eyes and the nose harmonizes with the coat color. The ears are large but not as long as the Cocker's and are set higher. The tail is low set, often with a lively action. The coat is short and glossy on the body and head, and thick, fairly long, and slightly wavy on the ears, chest, under the body, and on the back of the legs.

The color is usually white with black or liver markings. The height at the shoulder for dogs is about 20 inches, bitches are slightly smaller.

English Toy Spaniel, see **Cavalier King Charles Spaniel**

English Toy Terrier *Britain*

Known sometimes in Britain as the 'Black and Tan' (and in the United States as Toy Black and Tan or Toy Manchester Terrier), the English Toy Terrier is descended from the smooth-coated Manchester Terrier, which for centuries was used for ratting in the north of England. Although it was evolved in the nineteenth century, it is still not especially popular. Just why is difficult to understand since the breed is hardy and suited to small, modern houses, requires little exercise, has a trouble-free coat, and a modest appetite. This breed makes a loyal pet, but is not well suited to children.

The English Toy Terrier is elegantly and cleanly built. The head is flat and narrow with small eyes set fairly close together and with a keen, sparkling expression. The ears are erect. The tail is fairly long and thin and should not be carried above the level of the back. The coat is short and glossy.

The color is always black with chestnut-colored markings, which should be evenly distributed on the muzzle, cheeks, and the inside of the legs.

The height at the shoulder is 10 to 12 inches, and the ideal weight is 6 to 8 pounds.

Above right: English Toy Terrier.
Below: English Springer Spaniel.

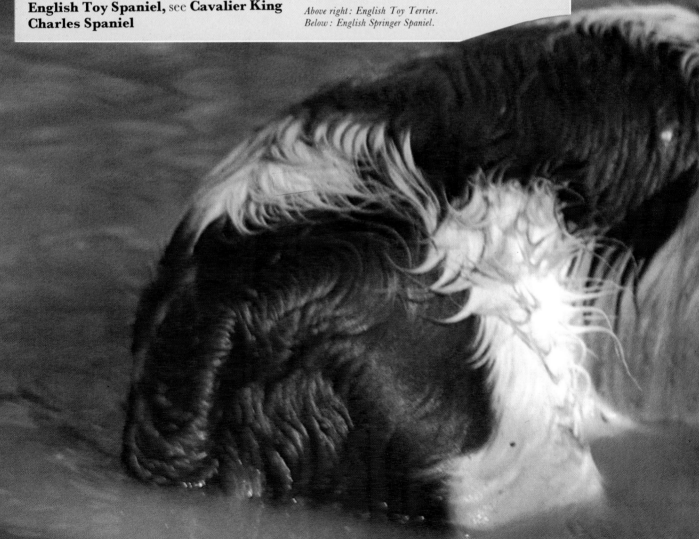

Entlebuch Mountain Dog *Switzerland*
The Swiss Entlebucher Sennenhund is a mountain dog that has been rescued from extinction in the course of this century. It was not officially recognized as a breed until comparatively recently and, although it is now popular in Switzerland, it is rare in other countries.

The Entlebuch Mountain Dog is the smallest of four Swiss 'sennen' (literally Alpine farm dog) breeds. It has a broad skull, dark eyes, and the ears, which are proportionally larger than those of the Bernese Mountain Dog, are carried close to the head. The neck is shorter and thicker, the body longer, and the legs considerably shorter than those of its close relatives. The tail is short.

The color is black with tan and white markings on the head, chest, and legs. The height at the shoulder is 16 to 20 inches.

Epagneul Bleu de Picardie and
Epagneul Picard *France*
The Epagneul Picard is the French Spaniel from Picardy which is widely used as a gundog in northern France. (The Epagneul Bleu de Picardie – the Blue Picardy Spaniel – is merely a color variety of the Epagneul Picard, having black markings on a blue merle base color in place of the Picard's tan patches.)

These French dogs differ from English spaniels insofar as they are lighter and leggier. The Epagneul Picard has a brown nose and dark amber-colored eyes, and the ears are set much higher than in most other spaniels. The tail is moderately long and is not docked. The coat is profuse – especially on the ears, chest, and tail – and slightly wavy at the tips. The hair on the head is slightly softer and finer than on the body.

The color is a grayish blue merle with chestnut-colored patches, especially on the head and feet. The height at the shoulder is 22 to 24 inches.

Epagneul Breton *France*
The Brittany Spaniel is the only spaniel in the world that 'points.' The French were first to produce the original dogs in the middle of the nineteenth century and started using them as pointing gundogs. They were not generally known outside France until the Americans adopted the breed; after that Brittany Spaniels were exported – from the USA as well as from France – to many different countries, and the breed is now represented all over the world. They are very agile sprinters, adaptable, and capable of great endurance.

The Brittany Spaniel is related to the old types of working spaniel which were imported into France from Great Britain. It is symmetrically built and on the same lines as modern English spaniels. The head is fairly broad, the ears are higher set than those of a Cocker Spaniel, and it is shorter in neck but longer in body and higher on the leg. The tail is short or nonexistent. The coat is thick and soft, but not too profuse except on ears, belly, and breeches where it forms attractive fringes.

The color is white with dark orange markings. The height at the shoulder is about 20 inches.

Epagneul Français *France*
This is the French Spaniel, which may not be as well known outside France as its British cousins, but it is just as old and basically it comes from the same stock. However, over the years the Epagneul Français has evolved into a spaniel which looks like something of a cross between the English Springer and the Cavalier King Charles Spaniel.

Its head is definitely spaniel type but plainer than that of the Cocker. The ears are set fairly high, the eyes are dark amber in color. The tail is not docked but is fairly long and is carried low or in line with the back. The coat is soft and abundant, slightly wavy, and well feathered on ears and tail.

The color is always white with chestnut markings. The average height at the shoulder for dogs is about 22 to 24 inches, for bitches 21 to 23 inches.

Right: Epagneul Bleu de Picardie.
Below: Epagneul Français.

Erdelyi Kopo *Hungary*

The Erdelyi Kopo is a Hungarian hound noted for its intelligence and obedience. There are two varieties – a long-legged breed used for wild-boar hunting, and a smaller type for hunting foxes and hares.

The Erdelyi Kopo has much in common with the Central European group of Foxhound and harrier-type hounds. It is almost rectangular in shape, with dark and slightly obliquely set eyes and high-set ears carried close to the head. The larger variety has a longer and thicker coat than its smaller relative. This larger type is usually black, the smaller red. The height at the shoulder is 22 to 26 inches and 18 to 20 inches respectively. Weights vary between 66 and 77 pounds.

Eskimo Dog *Canada*

The dog known simply as the Eskimo is a native of Canada and is very similar to the Greenland Dog; indeed it is debatable whether they should be regarded as two separate breeds. The Eskimo, which belongs to the polar spitz breeds, is used in the northern arctic wastelands to pull sleds. Generally it leads a very independent life, is left to forage for its own food, and is hardly ever kept indoors. But it can adjust to less rugged conditions and it is said that it can become very affectionate.

In conformation it is typical of the heavier and coarser spitz breeds – powerfully built with a bold, spirited expression. The head has a broad skull and the eyes are small, watchful, and slanting. The dog is strong, with well-boned legs and unusually large feet. The tail is short and tightly curled. The coat is very coarse, thick, and straight, and is particularly close on the body, tail, and in between the toes for protection against the cold. Any color and mixture of colors is acceptable. Minimum height at the shoulder for dogs is about 24 inches. Weight varies but is usually between 65 and 85 pounds.

Estrela Mountain Dog *Portugal*

This tough, independent working dog comes from the Estrela mountain district, and is able to withstand the rigors of climate and mountainous terrain. The breed is large and heavy and valued as a housedog and as a guard for livestock.

The Estrela has a powerful body in which the Mastiff influence can clearly be seen, although the head is lighter and less blunt in the foreface. It combines a firm and muscular back with a deep chest, slightly raised loins, and straight strong legs. Its long tail is carried low. The eyes are dark amber and the ears small, triangular, and dropped. The hair can be long or short, thick, rather coarse, smooth or slightly wavy. Colors are gray, tawny and red, red or light tan with white points, black and tan, black and white, red and tan, and grizzle. The weight is 90 to 110 pounds for males, and bitches are considerably lighter. The height is 23 to 27 inches.

Fauve de Bretagne *France*

The Fauve de Bretagne (literally Brittany fawn) is the Brittany Basset, evolved from crossing Griffons with Bassets. The Fauve de Bretagne is active and fast for its size. Its body shape is rectangular; the foreface is straight or very slightly convex. The eyes are dark and the ears are large and pendulous, the neck muscular and fairly short. The coat is very rough and close.

The color is either wheaten or gray, preferably without markings on the chest and feet. The height at the shoulder varies between 13 and 14 inches.

Below: Eskimo Dog. Below right: Fauve de Bretagne. Far right: Estrela Mountain Dog.

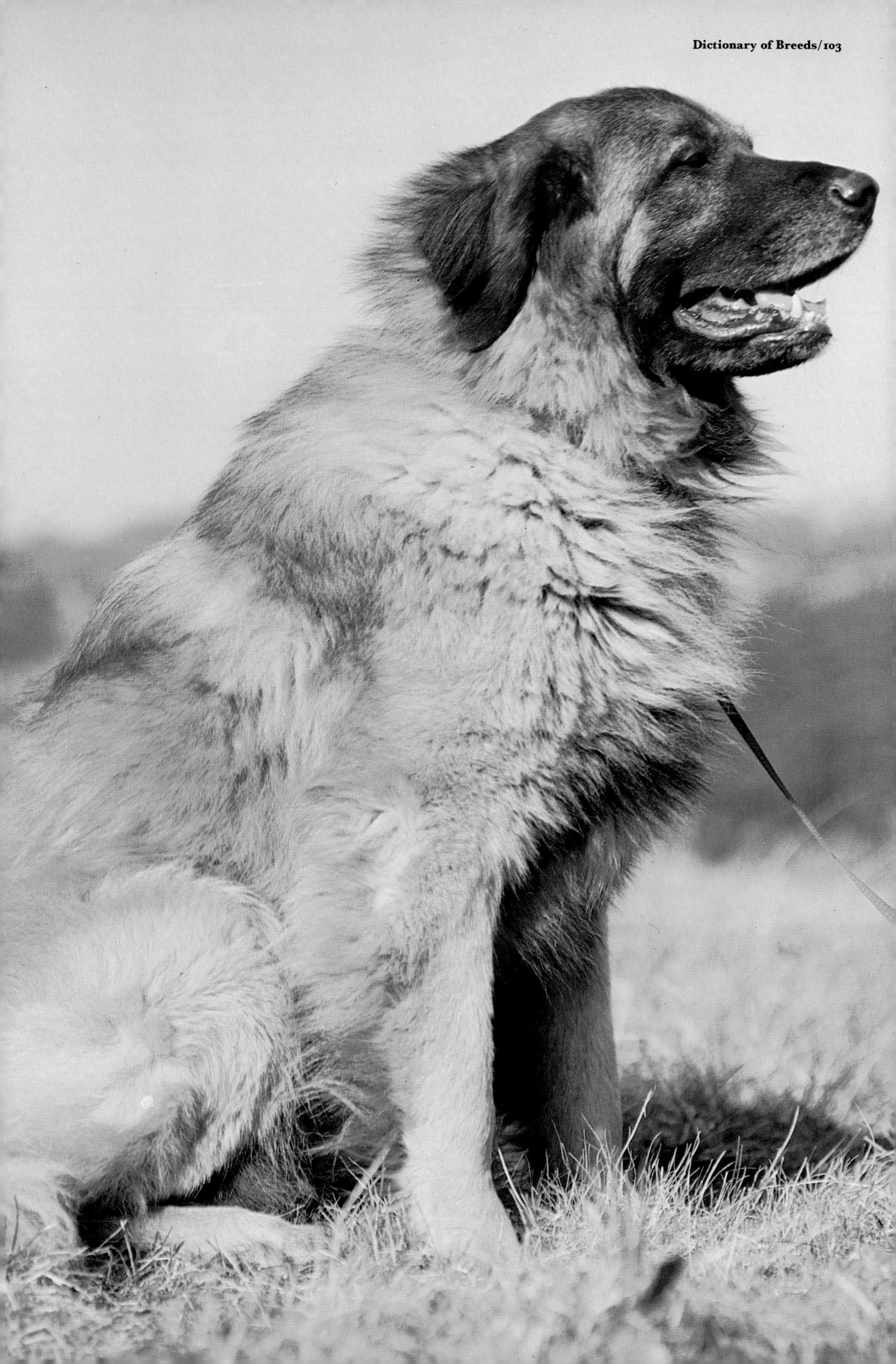

Field Spaniel *Britain*

The Field Spaniel shares the ancestry of the other spaniel breeds, but has remained a working breed and is normally seen at field trials rather than at formal dog shows.

It is a well-balanced sporting dog with a docile temperament. According to the breed standard it also has a 'grave' expression. The head is similar to that of the Cocker, but is not as distinctive and is really more like a setter's. The body and bone are lighter than the Cocker's and the coat is less profuse, forming silky feathering similar to an Irish Setter.

As in most other spaniel breeds, there are several color varieties, but black, black and tan, roan, or solid-color shades of liver are preferable to particolors. The height at the shoulder is about 18 inches

Fila Brasileiro *Brazil*

The Fila Brasileiro is the Brazilian Mastiff, and it is directly descended from the Spanish Mastiffs which accompanied the conquistadors to South America in the sixteenth century. It may therefore be considered a cousin of the Mastin Español.

The Fila Brasileiro is a powerful and imposing animal with a well-boned frame and a heavy head. The hindquarters appear to be slightly higher than the forequarters, while the tail, which is thick at the root, tapers toward the tip. The eyes are dark, the ears fairly large and hanging. The coat is short, close, and soft.

The Fila Brasileiro is brindle or self-colored in any color, but white markings are confined to the feet and the tip of the tail. It usually has a black mask and black ears. The average size is 15 to 20 inches.

Finnish Spitz *Finland*

The Finnish Spitz (Suomenpystykorva) is

Below: Field Spaniel.

virtually unknown outside Finland. In its home country it is the most popular breed, and recently has become more popular as a pet in other Scandinavian countries.

It is a lively hunter and has all the spitz characteristics: a firmly knit body, bold bearing, and a lively temperament. The eyes sparkle and the ears are mobile and sharply pointed. The body is short and lithe, the legs straight with a springy action, and the tail curves vigorously in an arch against the thigh. The coat is profuse, fairly long, very straight, and is especially long on the neck, back, tail, and thighs.

The color is a bright reddish-brown or yellowish-red with lighter shadings – preferably without a narrow white stripe on the breast or white markings on the feet. Particolors are not acceptable. The height at the shoulder is $17\frac{1}{2}$ to 20 inches for dogs, $15\frac{1}{2}$ to 18 inches for bitches.

Finnish Stövare *Finland*

The Finnish Stövare (Suomenajokoira) has a mixed ancestry, including the old hunting dogs which also sired the Swedish 'stövare' varieties and a number of 'immigrant' breeds – notably from Russia. Physically it is similar to the Hamiltonstövare, for which it is sometimes mistaken; but is generally slightly taller and its shape more rectangular.

The Finnish Stövare is not heavy yet it is powerful. Nevertheless it has a very docile, alert temperament. The occiput is more pronounced than in the Hamiltonstövare; the foreface is long, strong, and finely chiselled. The eyes are dark and the ears are carried close to the head; the coat is close and fairly hard.

The color is tan with a black saddle and white markings on the foreface, neck, chest, feet, and tip of the tail. The height at the shoulder is 20 to 24 inches.

Right: Finnish Spitz.

Flat-coated Retriever *Britain*
This is a fairly uncommon gundog breed –
distinguished, of course, by its flat coat.
(Other retrievers have wavy coats, as
indeed did this breed in its infancy.)
Although it is a true British dog, its
ancestors are believed to have been Newfoundland dogs which accompanied Canadian seafarers to British ports; later these
dogs were interbred with setters and
pointers. But it is the Labrador Retriever
which is thought to have been responsible
for the evolution of the flat coat.

The Flat-coated Retriever is a powerful
animal, yet it does not give the appearance
of being either cumbersome or lanky. The
eyes are hazel or dark brown and the
ears are small and carried close to the side
of the head. The coat is close, fine in
texture, and should be as flat as possible.
Fore- and hindquarters are well feathered.

The color is black or liver. The height at
the shoulder is about 23 inches and the
weight between 60 and 70 pounds.

Fox Terrier *Britain*
Basically there are two categories of Fox
Terrier – the wire-haired breed and the
Smooth Fox Terrier. However, at the turn
of the century, American dog fanciers
began to breed a miniature, or toy,
variety of the Smooth Fox Terrier and in
the United States the breed is now recognized as having a separate status.

In effect the Wire-haired Fox Terrier is
generally regarded as *the* terrier. This is
because of its temperament and attitude,
for it embodies all the typical terrier-like
characteristics – keenness and alertness
coupled with a slight aggressiveness. These
features have made it one of the most
popular breeds in the world. The Wire-

haired Fox Terrier is square built and
energetic. Its coat is wiry with abundant
whiskers and leg hair. White predominates,
but otherwise color is of little importance.
Dogs stand just over 15 inches at the
shoulder with a weight of about 18 pounds;
bitches are proportionally smaller and
lighter.

The Smooth Fox Terrier is believed to
have evolved from crosses between its
wire-haired relative and other dogs used
for hunting foxes. Its temperament differs
from that of the wire-haired terrier insofar
as it is less boisterous. Nevertheless, today
it is probably as popular as the wire-haired
dog. In appearance – apart from the coat –
very little separates the two varieties, but
the head tapers slightly more from the
ears toward the eyes and the muzzle is
slightly more pointed. The coat should be
smooth, thick, and close; the belly and
underside of the thighs should be covered.
Color, height, and weight are the same as
for the Wire-haired Fox Terrier.

Finally, the essentials of the American
Toy Fox Terrier have been defined as:
weight between $3\frac{1}{2}$ and 7 pounds (dogs over
7 pounds are not considered as being in the
toy class), color is usually white with black
and tan markings, ears are carried erect;
the muzzle is narrow but relatively long;
and the tail should be docked fairly short.

French Bulldog, see **Bouledogue
Français**

French Spaniel, see **Epagneul Français**

Above far right: Smooth-haired Fox Terrier.
Above right: Wire-haired Fox Terrier.
Right: Wire-haired Fox Terrier puppies.
Below: Flat-coated Retriever.

German Shepherd *Germany*

The Deutsche Schäferhund, commonly known in Britain and most of the Commonwealth countries as the Alsatian, is probably the most internationally popular breed. And over the years it has had more publicity, good and bad, than all the other breeds of dogs put together. The Alsatian possesses highly developed senses mentally and temperamentally, and this makes it ideally suited to training in a variety of fields – with the police, the armed forces, and the blind. However, the same qualities that make it an admirable working dog make it equally unsuitable in the wrong hands, and one often reads of attacks on the breed when Alsatians are accused of treachery, savagery, sheep killing, and the like. (The import of Alsatians into Australia is prohibited.)

The Alsatian did not become a breed in the real sense until the latter half of the nineteenth century, and the way it looks today is the result of only a few decades of intensive and skillful German breeding.

Predominantly native breeds form the foundation of the Alsatian, from pure spitz breed types to dogs on sheepdog lines.

According to the breed standard, the Alsatian is active, alert, and good natured. The color is usually shades of gray to black with even, lighter markings. White or near white are not considered desirable. The height at the shoulder for dogs is 24 to 26 inches, for bitches 22 to 24 inches.

German Short-haired Pointer *Germany*

The Deutscher Vorstehhund, Kurzhaar, is the equivalent of the English Pointer. It is one of the best-known sporting dogs in the world and is equally popular in the United States.

The ancestry of both the German and British breeds is the same – French and Spanish gun dogs. However, the English variety got a dash of Foxhound, while the German pointers gained from some crossing with some heavier breeds. Sportsmen appreciate the dog that has evolved not only for its ability to find, 'point-up,' flush,

and retrieve game, but also because of the German pointer's willingness to face sleet and cold rain, heavy cover, and to go into cold, rough water to retrieve a duck.

A German Short-haired Pointer is classy without being too elegant and powerful without being too heavy. The ears are soft and hang close to the head; the nose is solid brown. The back is slightly sloping, the chest well developed, and the legs muscular with well-bent stifles. The tail is docked to medium length, about two-thirds from the root. The coat is thick and short but fairly coarse. Except for a longer coat, the Long-haired Pointer is identical.

The color is liver, liver and white spotted, or liver and white ticked. Dogs stand 23 to 25 inches at the shoulder, bitches 21 to 23 inches. Dogs weigh 55 to 70 pounds.

German Wire-haired Pointer *Germany*
Although the modern Deutscher Vorsteh-hund, Drahthaar, looks, apart from the coat, very like the short-haired variety, its background is rather different. Wire-haired

German gundogs are mentioned in medieval literature, but not until this century were German Wire-haired Pointers recognized as a breed. The reason for this is that the breed was developed by crossing the offspring of a number of other breeds – the Wire-haired Pointing Griffon, the Stichelhaar (a retriever), the Pudel-pointer (Poodle Pointer), the German Short-haired Pointer, and possibly the English Pointer. The result was that it was some time before a true breed emerged and, until it did, the various types competed against each other to find favor with sportsmen.

Except for the coat, the German Wire-haired conforms to the standard of the short-haired variety. The coat is rough and close all over except on the ears, eyebrows, and jaws where it is more profuse, giving it busy eyebrows, beard, and whiskers. The height for dogs is 24 to 26 inches, and bitches not less than 22 inches.

Far left: German Shepherd.
Center: German Long-haired Pointer.
Below: German Short-haired Pointer.

Golden Retriever *Britain*

The Golden Retriever is a delightful and adaptable animal equally capable of becoming a first-class gundog, a good-natured companion, or a conscientious guide dog for the blind. Since the end of World War II it has become increasingly popular as a pet because of its friendly temperament.

The origin of the breed dates back to the second half of the nineteenth century and there is a popular account of how the Golden Retriever came to be. According to this story, in 1858 a certain Sir Dudley Marjoribanks saw an act put on by a troop of Russian tracker dogs at a travelling circus performance in Brighton. Impressed with the cleverness and appearance of these dogs, he decided to acquire a pair of them, but ended up purchasing the lot. The dogs were then duly taken to Sir Dudley's estate in Scotland, bred from, and laid the foundation of the breed.

Unfortunately this story is fiction, not fact. In 1952 the kennel records of Sir Dudley's estate from 1835 to 1890 were published and from these it became clear that the breed we now know as Golden Retrievers came from a yellow dog bred from Flat-coated Retriever parents mated to a little liver-colored English Retriever; the Russian acrobats never came into the picture. The Flat-coated Retriever sire was called Nous and the litter produced by his diminutive mate consisted of four puppies, whose names are given as Crocus, Primrose, Cowslip, and Ada. In the event the direct progeny of this union proved to be excellent gundogs, the strain was largely kept pure, and by the beginning of this century the Golden Retriever began to establish itself.

The Golden Retriever is a well-proportioned dog, active, docile, powerful, and yet stylish. The coat is either flat or wavy, close, water-resistant, and with good feathering, especially on the tail.

The color may be any shade of gold or cream, neither too dark nor too light. Dogs stand 22 to 24 inches at the shoulder, bitches 20 to 22 inches, while weight is about 67 and 57 pounds respectively.

Gontjaja Estonskaja, Gontjaja Ruskaja, Gontjaja Ruskaja Pegaja *USSR*

Few people on the western side of the Iron Curtain appreciate that there is a Soviet canine world, and that there are breeds other than the Borzoi and the Laika. One of the most popular breeds in Russia is in fact the Foxhound type, of which the Gontjaja Ruskaja is the most common.

This breed and the European Stövare group probably share the same ancestors, but over the years it has developed its own characteristics and is now considerably heavier and thicker set than most of its relations. The head is cone-shaped with a well-set foreface and fairly long ears carried close to the head. The tail is long and thick, gradually tapering toward the tip. The coat is short and hard.

The color is brownish black with lighter shadings. The height at the shoulder is 22 to 24 inches.

The Gontjaja Ruskaja Pegaja, a particolored variety, is similar to the Gontjaja Ruskaja but it is less common, and at dog shows in Moscow it is reported that only about half as many Ruskaja Pegajas are likely to be shown as Gontjaja Ruskajas. (Even more rare are the Gontjaja Estonskajas. Only two or three of the Estonskaja variety would be entered.) The body color of the Pegaja is white or cream with large tan patches, and either with or without a black saddle. (Too much white is apparently not desirable.) It is slightly taller than the Gontjaja Ruskaja, often 24 inches at the shoulder – and it has shorter ears and tail.

Finally the Estonskaja is similar in type to its cousins but is slightly longer and shorter-legged. In color it is generally particolor or tricolor.

Gordon Setter *Britain*

The Gordon Setter is the only gundog evolved in Scotland, despite that country's sporting background. At one time it was the most popular of all pointing gundogs, but when the English Setter appeared on the scene the number of Gordon Setters in Britain declined. Although it has regained some of its popularity in recent years, in 1962 registrations in England were down to a mere 28. In America the figures are better.

The Gordon Setter is slightly larger than the English Setter and does not have quite the same elegant appearance. The ears are soft and lie close to the head. The tail is fairly short and straight, and in action is carried horizontally or below the line of the back. The coat is short and fine, but forms long and silky featherings on the ears, belly, tail, and back of legs.

The color is always black with smaller chestnut-red markings on the muzzle, chest, and underside of the body. A white spot on the chest is allowed, but not desirable. The height at the shoulder is about 26 inches for dogs and about 24 inches for bitches. The weight (dogs) is about 65 pounds (UK), and 55 to 80 pounds (USA).

Right: Gordon Setter.

Grand Bleu de Gascogne *France*

The Grand Bleu de Gascogne is one of the oldest hound breeds. It is descended from the ancient Phoenician Harrier/Foxhound types which in medieval times were crossed with Bloodhounds. It is likely that it was established as a breed as early as the sixteenth century and it is believed to have been very popular; it was even used by the royal hunting parties and was highly praised for its good nose. As distinct from many other old French hunting breeds, the Grand Bleu de Gascogne has survived and prospered, and even contributed to the formation of other new breeds like the Petit Bleu de Gascogne and Basset Bleu de Gascogne.

The 'big blue' is a tall, elegant dog with a long head and large, pendulous ears. The chest is deep and the tail long, sometimes with a flag underneath. The coat, though not at all coarse, should not be too short and smooth.

The 'blue' color is really a mass of small black markings on a white background, giving a merle impression. There are larger black patches on the head and sometimes on the body. The height at the shoulder is 25 to 28 inches for dogs, 24 to 26 inches for bitches.

Grand Griffon Vendéen *France*

The 'Grand' Vendéen is a French sporting dog, the largest of four varieties of Vendéen Griffons taking their name from the French department of Vendée. Originally it was used for hunting wolves, but with the virtual demise of that sport it was used mainly for tracking game.

The Grand Griffon Vendéen is extremely powerful and robust. The head is long and fairly narrow with powerful jaws. The eyes are large, dark, and keen, the ears soft, pendulous, and fairly long. The tail is relatively high and carried 'saber-fashion but not as a scythe,' as the breed standard states. The coat is coarse and fairly long with particularly abundant moustaches and eyebrows.

The color may be white with red, fawn, or gray markings, fawn, 'hare-colored,' or tricolor. The height at the shoulder is 24 to 26 inches.

Great Dane *Germany*

The breed known as the Great Dane *may* have originated in Denmark – hence the name linking it with that country. There is no doubt that it was in Germany that the breed reached its present standard of excellence, and the German name – Deutsche Dogge, or German Mastiff – would have been a more suitable designation. Its ancestors were the heavy Mastiff-type war dogs attached to Caesar's Roman legions. Their progeny were used by continental noblemen for hunting, and in the eighteenth and nineteenth centuries no German *Schloss* (castle) was considered complete without one or more imposing Deutsche Dogges. Bismarck, the Iron Chancellor, kept them as bodyguards and pets and was said to be especially fond of them.

The ideal Great Dane is a combination of strength and elegance. Viewed from the side, the head, which is carried proudly, is broad and deep with a pronounced stop and a deep muzzle. The ears may be carried close to the head or cropped. The coat is short and sleek. The minimum height of an adult dog should be 30 inches, that of a bitch 28 inches. The minimum weight for dogs is 120 pounds, bitches 100 pounds.

Below left: Grand Bleu de Gascogne.
Below right: Grand Griffon Vendéen.
Right: Great Dane.

Greenland Dog *Greenland*
The Gronlandshund, a sledge dog used by the Eskimos, is another of the polar spitz breeds similar in conformation to the Canadian Eskimo Dog. Also see *Eskimo Dog*.

Greyhound *Britain*
Greyhounds have been with us and used for coursing game for centuries – certainly from Roman times, if not earlier. (Bas-reliefs on the tombs of Egyptian pharaohs show dogs that bear a remarkable resemblance to the modern Greyhound.) More-over, it appears that over the centuries they have retained a greater purity of form than most other breeds.

The name greyhound probably derives from the fact that gray was at one time the most usual color for dogs of this breed, but it is also possible that it may come from 'gaze' – a word which was descriptive of a dog which hunts by sight. The latter would be more appropriate because the Greyhound was employed until modern times for coursing deer, stag, gazelle, fox, and hare. In feudal Britain the possession of Greyhounds was an upper-class status symbol, restricted to the landed gentry, and according to the law 'No meane person may keep Greyhounds.' An old Welsh proverb made the point, 'You may know a gentleman by his horse, his hawk, and his Greyhound.'

Since World War I the Greyhound has generally been restricted to an artificial

Above left: Griffon Brabaçon.
Above: Greyhounds.

form of coursing – on the racetrack. Greyhound racing continues to be immensely
popular but in recent years the Greyhound
has come to be appreciated as a pet – a
role for which, because of its gentle and
affectionate nature, it is ideally suited.

The Greyhound is a classy, muscular,
and supple dog. All colors are acceptable
in any shade from black to white, self-
colored or particolored. The height at the
shoulder is between 28 and 30 inches for
dogs, and between 27 and 28 inches for
bitches. The weight for dogs is 65 to 70
pounds, bitches 60 to 65 pounds.

Griffon Belge *Belgium*
The Belgian Griffon differs from the
more common Griffon Bruxellois in color
only: it is black and tan, pure black, or
grizzle.

Griffon Brabançon *Belgium*
Two varieties of Belgian Griffons are
recognized today: the Brabançon, better
known as the Smooth Griffon, and the
Rough Griffon, whose correct name is
Brussels Griffon (Griffon Bruxellois). As
may be deduced from the Anglicized
names, the Brabançon has a smooth coat
while the Bruxellois has a coarse one. With
the exception of the coat, which in the
Griffon Brabançon is short and smooth, the
two varieties are identical. Both roughs and
smooths are often born in the same litter.

Griffon Bruxellois *Belgium*
The Brussels Griffon is the variety now better known as the Rough Griffon. Its ancestry is very mixed, but the breed probably started off as a variation of the now fairly rare breed of German Affenpinscher farm dog. Initially they were kept as ratters on farms and in the stables which housed the fiacres or hansom cabs. However, their self-assertiveness and determination to be with their owners at all times led to them travelling round on the front seat of the fiacres, from where it was a short step to a position in society as fashionable pets. Once established as such, other breeds were brought in to 'smarten' them up; these appear to have included a variety of terriers, pugs and – judging by the Brussels Griffon's large, expressive eyes – toy spaniels.

The Griffon Bruxellois is a compact, sturdy, and lively dog with an alert and cheeky expression. The head is large with a short, wide muzzle and a slightly undershot mouth, without showing the teeth or tongue. The eyes are large and dark, the ears very small and semierect. The coat is rough and straight, forming an abundant beard on the chin.

The color is either red, black, or black and tan. White patches are highly undesirable. Weight varies considerably, but should preferably be between 3 and 10 pounds. The breed standard does not specify height.

Griffon Fauve de Bretagne *France*
This is the fawn Griffon from Brittany, which in medieval times was reputedly used for hunting wolves. The breed is now very rare, even in Brittany.

The Brittany Griffon is of medium size, very muscular, and well boned. The eyes are dark and expressive, the nose black or brown. The ears are pendulous and long enough to be capable of being extended beyond the tip of the nose. The back is short and broad. The tail is of medium length with a slight curve at the end and is carried in line with the back. The coat, which should not be long and never woolly, is exceedingly coarse.

The color is fawn, preferably in shades of golden or reddish brown. The height at the shoulder is 20 to 22 inches for dogs, 19 to 21 inches for bitches.

Griffon Nivernois *France*
The Nivernais Griffon takes its name from the French province where it is said to have originated. In former times it was used for wild boar hunting, and the fact that wild boars are rarely hunted these days probably accounts for the current scarcity of the Nivernais Griffon. Although it is said to be an affectionate dog – rather as the Bloodhound is affectionate – its coarse and rugged appearance makes it an unattractive pet.

As a hunting dog it was valued more for its strength, courage, and stamina than for its speed. It is now a fairly thick-set, heavy animal with a rectangular body and mournful expression. The head is fairly small in relation to the body. The eyes are preferably dark and expressive, the ears pendulous. The tail is of moderate length and it may occasionally be slightly curled at the tip. The coat is profuse and coarse without curl.

The color is preferably wolf gray or slate blue, but may also be black with or without tan markings, or even fawn. The height at the shoulder is between 21 and 23 inches for dogs, proportionally less for bitches.

Groenendael, see **Belgian Shepherd**

Grosser Münsterländer *Germany*
See *Münsterländer*. The large (Grosser) variety is very similar to the more common, smaller Münsterländer. However, its color is usually white with black markings; all black is less desirable. The height at the shoulder is 23 to 25 inches. It is about 4 inches taller than its smaller relation.

Right: Grosser Munsterländer.
Below: Griffon Bruxellois.

Hairless dogs

In Western countries hairless dogs are generally regarded as canine curiosities. Some kennel clubs have claimed that hairless dogs are not a breed but monstrosities within a breed. However, such dogs do exist, and as a rule they all come from tropical or semitropical countries.

The best-known varieties are the Chinese Crested Dog and the Mexican Hairless Dog. Their most marked characteristic is the total absence of coat. The cause of this is not known; it has been attributed to a blood factor deficiency, to a skin ailment, and to malfunctioning genes. Missing teeth also appear to be linked with hairlessness. Sometimes all but the front teeth are missing, but usually only the premolars are missing. In litters of both breeds an occasional puppy is born with normal hair and teeth; it is called a 'powder puff.'

Oddly enough, the Mexican Hairless is not recognized in Mexico, and the American Kennel Club has withdrawn its recognition of the breed. (Mexico recognizes one hairless breed, the Xoloitzcuintli – supposedly the descendant of dogs kept by the Aztecs.) Canada, which does still recognize the breed, calls for a dog slightly smaller than the Fox Terrier, with erect, rounded ears and a smooth, totally hairless body – except for a topknot between the ears.

The breed standard for the Chinese Crested Dog is similar, except that hair is permitted on the skull, feet, and tip of the tail. Color may vary with both breeds according to the climate. It can be elephant gray, gray with unpigmented flesh-colored patches, or liver with gray or black patches. The weight can be anything between 8 and 16 pounds.

Haldenstövare *Norway*

Although it is classified as a Scandinavian harrier/foxhound, the Norwegian Haldenstövare stems mainly from British stock. Foxhounds from Britain were combined with Norwegian varieties to develop a breed that was not recognized until the 1950s. The Haldenstövare is usually slightly smaller than its British ancestor, but it looks very much like a foxhound. It is heavily built and has a placid disposition. The head resembles the foxhound's, with a slightly tapering foreface and large, soft ears. The eyes are dark brown, the neck long, and the body strong and powerful.

The color is usually white with black patches and smaller tan markings on the head and the legs. The height at the shoulder is 20 to 24 inches.

Right: Chinese Crested Dog. Far right: Xoloitzcuintli. Far right above: Powder Puff with Chinese Crested Dog.

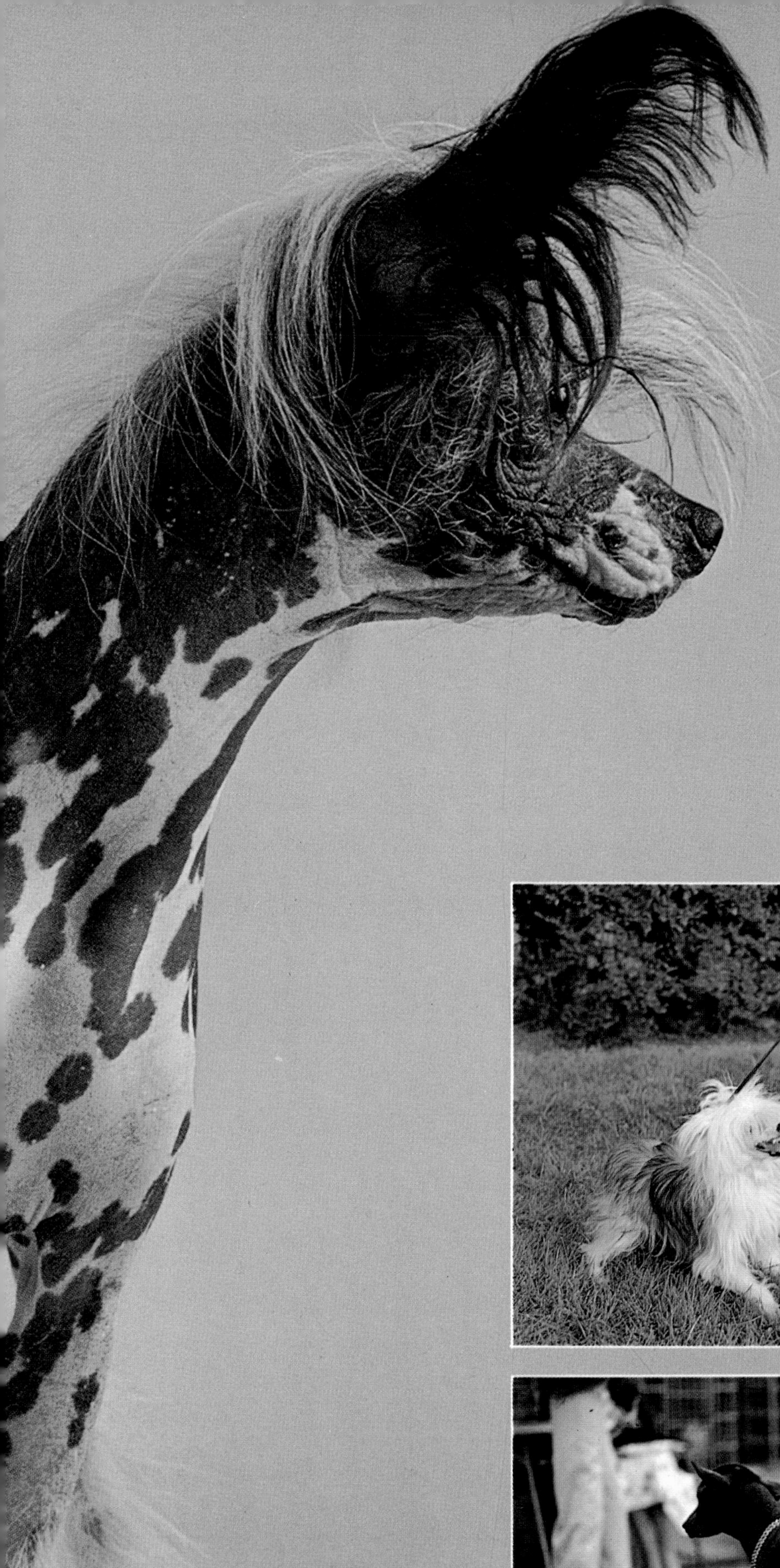

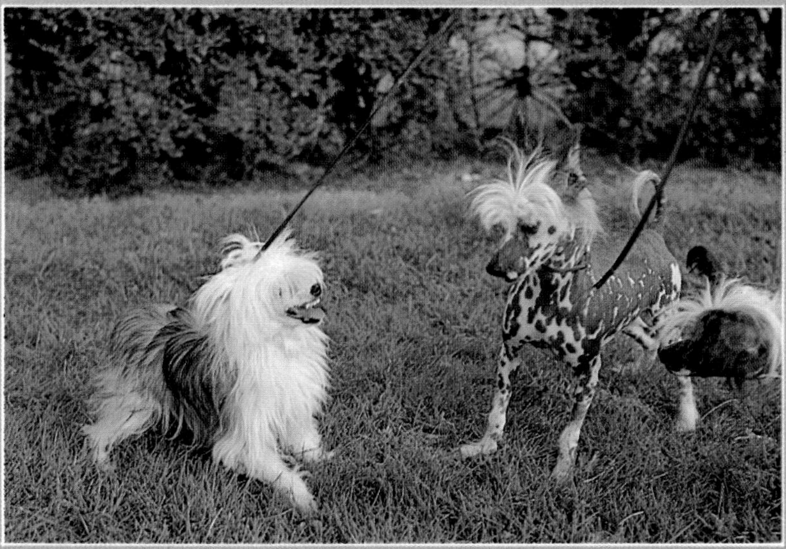

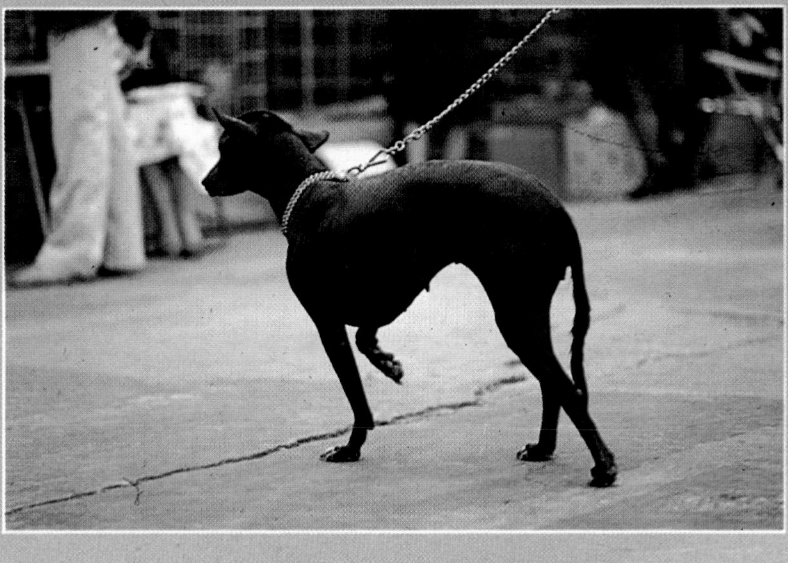

Hamiltonstövare *Sweden*

This breed is rare outside Scandinavia but in Sweden the Hamiltonstövare is one of the most popular of the hunting breeds. For centuries it has been bred specifically for Swedish hunting conditions. Like the Haldenstövare, the Hamiltonstövare originates from foreign hounds – mainly imports from Britain, Germany, and Switzerland.

It is a powerful and agile dog. The head is cleanly cut with a full, fairly long foreface. The eyes are clear and dark brown. The ears are fairly large and soft and are carried close to the head. The tail is either straight or very slightly wavy; the coat is close.

The Hamiltonstövare is always tricolor: tan predominates, with a black saddle and white markings on the muzzle, throat, chest, feet, and tip of the tail. The height at the shoulder for dogs is 20 to 24 inches, 18 to 22 inches for bitches.

Hanoverian Schweisshund *Germany*

Because of its sensitive nose and quiet and tranquil disposition, the Hannoveranischer Schweisshund is used for tracking wounded game.

It is a sturdy, low-set dog with a heavy head, a slightly wrinkled forehead, and very broad muzzle. The ears are long, without folds, and carried close to the head.

The color is grayish brown or red with darker markings on the muzzle, above the eyes, and on the ears. White or light markings are not acceptable. The height at the shoulder varies considerably between dogs and bitches: the dog may be up to 24 inches, while the bitch is normally about 18 inches.

Harlekinpinscher *Germany*

The Harlequin Pinscher is closely related to and descended from the Pinscher. However, it differs in its smaller size and color: it is predominantly white or light in color with darker, sometimes brindle, even patches.

The height at the shoulder is 12 to 14 inches.

Harrier *Britain*

The Harrier takes its name from the Norman-Saxon word 'Harier,' which means a general hunting dog. In 1750 the breed was divided into two varieties, the Staghound and the Dwarf Foxhound. At the end of the eighteenth century, when English sportsmen took to hunting hares, the Harrier was found to be particularly well suited to it, partly because of its size. The breed is now very rare, even in Britain, and is not officially recognized by the Kennel Club.

Dogs which might be classified as Harriers were introduced to the USA and Canada prior to the War of Independence, but there are no true hares in New England and these small hounds were not fast enough to track the wily American fox.

In appearance the Harrier resembles a smaller version of its relative, the Foxhound. It is a smooth-haired dog of medium size with dropped ears and a long tail. The coat is short, hard, and close. The color is the same as the Foxhound: usually tan with a black saddle and white markings, or white with lemon markings. The height at the shoulder is 19 to 21 inches.

Hollandse Herdershond *Netherlands*

The Hollandse Herdershond is the equivalent of the French Berger varieties and the Belgian Groenendael and Tervueren, and to a lesser extent the German Shepherd (Alsatian). But while in France the varieties have been separated and given their own names, there is only one herding breed in the Netherlands. Yet within this breed there are three varieties, distinguished only by their coats. The smooth-haired (Kortharig) is the most common, next is the wire-haired (Steilharig) variety, and finally the long-haired (Langharig) which is now comparatively rare. Very few Hollandse Herdershonds are found outside the Netherlands.

Accepted colors are fawn, red, and brown; the smooth-haired variety is often cream or light and dark golden brindle, while the wire-haired Herdershond may be grayish blue or pepper and salt. The height at the shoulder may vary between 23 and 25 inches for dogs, and about 1 inch less for bitches.

Hound

This is a generic term for a dog which is used to hunt by tracking or by sight.

Hovawart *Germany*

The Hovawart derives its name from the German words for farm (*hof*) and watch (*wart*), and it is, as the name implies, a guard dog used on farms. It hails from southern Germany and is rarely seen outside its native region. However, in recent years it has gained some popularity in Britain.

The Hovawart is a big dog with a large and rounded head with drooping ears; the legs are straight and the long tail has a flag. The coat is wavy with a soft undercoat.

The color may be golden, black with brown markings, or possibly light brindle. The height at the shoulder is 24 to 28 inches for dogs, 22 to 26 inches for bitches.

Hrvatski Ovcar *Yugoslavia*
The Hrvatski Ovcar is a Croatian sheepdog
– a spitz-type with erect, pointed ears. It is,
however, longer in body than most other
spitz breeds and may be naturally tailless
or docked. The coat is thick and slightly
wavy on the body, profuse on the back of
the thighs and around the neck, but short
on the head, legs, and feet. The color is
usually black, but small white markings
are sometimes found.

The height at the shoulder for both dogs
and bitches varies from 16 to 20 inches.

Hungarian Kuvasz, see **Kuvasz**

Hungarian Puli, see **Puli**

Hungarian Vizsla, see **Vizsla**

Husky *USA*
The term husky usually implies an Arctic-
type dog of impure breeding, that is, a
mongrel. Thus one hears of Greenland
Huskies, Alaskan Huskies, and so on, such
dogs being neither Alaskan Malamutes nor
Siberian Huskies. The Siberian Husky is
the only pure breed entitled to include
Husky in its name. See *Siberian Husky.*

Below : Hamiltonstövare.

Hygenhund *Norway*

The Norwegian Hygenhund is closely related to the Norwegian Dunkerstövare, and there has been so much interbreeding of the two breeds that they are now almost indistinguishable. The true Hygenhund is red fawn in color, but the interbreeding has produced a black variety.

The main difference between the black varieties of the Hygenhund and Dunkerstövare is that the Hygenhund is slightly heavier. The head is broad with a marked stop and a wide foreface, which is slightly shorter than the Dunkerstövare's. The color of the eyes should harmonize with the coat color, but they should never be light-colored. The ears are thin and supple, the coat thick, flat, and glossy.

The color varies; tan, black and tan, or white with tan and/or black markings are all acceptable. The height at the shoulder is 19 to 24 inches.

Ibizan Hound *Spain*

The Ibizan Hound (Podenco Ibicenco) takes its name from the Balearic island of Ibiza, where it is said to have originated – although it is claimed that the best examples of the breed are found on the neighboring island of Majorca, where they are used to hunt hares and partridges. This breed hunts more by scent and hearing than by sight, and will bark only when a quarry is sensed. Three types of Ibizan Hound exist: smooth-haired, wire-haired, and long-haired. They are strongly built, very agile, very astute, intelligent, and docile, and they can jump to a great height without a take-off run.

The Ibizan Hound is white with red or fawn patches, or self-colored in any of these colors. The eyes are amber and the nose liver-colored. The height at the shoulder for dogs is 24 to 26 inches, 22 to 25 inches for bitches.

Iceland Dog *Iceland*

The Iceland Dog is a spitz type resembling the Norwegian Buhund. Its ancestors were probably taken to Iceland by sailors and immigrants to the country from Greenland, Finland, and Norway over a thousand years ago, but a series of recurring epidemics almost wiped out the breed until the Icelanders introduced dog-control legislation in the nineteenth century. The Iceland Dog had proved to be of exceptional worth to the country's farmers and they were determined to save the breed from extinction. Primarily these animals are used to herd sheep and, because of the Icelandic terrain, they have to use great care and intelligence bringing sheep down from the mountains.

In 1900 the Iceland Dog was recognized by the Danish Kennel Club and 15 years later by the British Kennel Club. The dog itself is slightly under middle size and lightly built. The head is light, broad between the ears, with a domed skull. The nose is black; the ears, large at the base, are triangular, pointed, and erect; the eyes small, round, and dark. The neck is short, the shoulders straight not sloping. The back is short, the chest large and deep. The tail is of moderate length, very bushy, and carried curled over the back. The coat is hard and of medium length. The color is white with fawn markings, golden, or light fawn with black tips to long hairs. The height is 15 to 18 inches and the weight about 30 pounds.

Illyrian Hound *Yugoslavia*

The Illyrian Hound is a powerful, heavily built dog used for hunting wild boars, foxes, and hares, rarely found outside its native country. Its general conformation is rectangular with a broad head, long pendulous ears, and a tail which curves slightly. Its coat is coarse and hard. The color may be white, fawn, tan, or gray with smaller markings, especially on the ears, in a contrasting color. The height at the shoulder is about 18 to 22 inches.

Irish Setter *Britain*

Some call him the Red Setter or the Irish Red Setter; in Britain and the United States he is known officially just as the Irish Setter. The rich chestnut color of the Irish Setter's coat is such a jealously preserved characteristic that the Irish formed a breed club over a century ago to protect the pure red color from any intermingling of blood from particolored dogs.

Unfortunately, the latter type proved to be more useful as gundogs, and the preference of the Irish for a pure red dog meant that their setter became less widely used than the particolored dogs. But the Irish Setter has retained its great attraction, and in the United States it is now one of the most fashionable show dogs.

With its striking color and its dark, expressive eyes combined with a lively and friendly temperament, the Irish Setter is possibly the most attractive of all the pointing gundog breeds. The coat is sleek, longer on the ears, chest, tail, and back of legs.

The color is always a glossy, rich chestnut with no trace of other shades. The height at the shoulder is usually about 24 inches and the weight is around 55 pounds.

Right: Ibizan Hound.
Above right: Irish Setter.

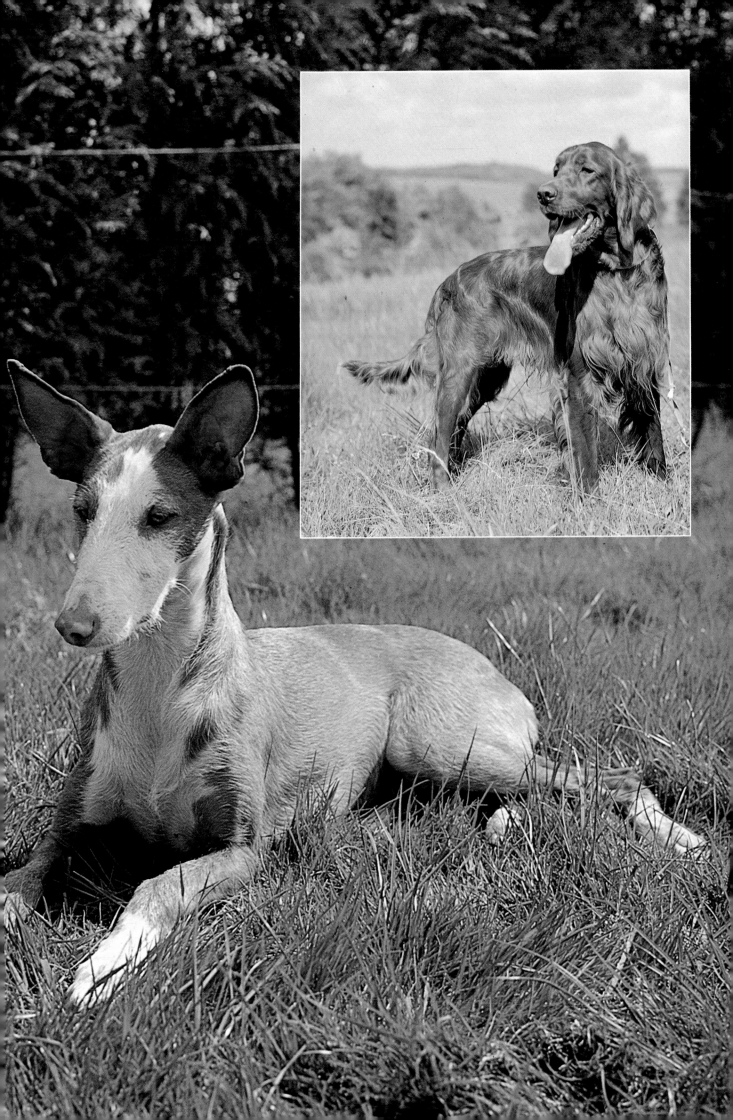

Irish Terrier *Britain*

The Irish Terrier is a comparatively recent breed whose popularity soared at the beginning of this century following an article on the breed in a work called *The Book of the Dog*. The writer of this article, a certain Mr Krehl, was an Irish Terrier enthusiast and he claimed that 'Micks' or 'Dare Devils,' as he termed the breed, could do anything any other dog could do, and do it better. According to him they were brilliant at ratting, rabbiting, and fox hunting; they excelled as gundogs, would work hedgerows like spaniels, retrieve like Labradors or quarter the ground like pointers and setters – they were even-tempered, courageous, trainable, and hardy. The truth, of course, is that the 'Irish' are typical terriers; they are inquisitive and venturesome, and they make ideal companions. In size the Irish Terriers are midway between the Welsh or Lakeland terriers and the Airedale. Yet, in spite of their terrier qualities and convenient size, they have never quite caught on either as a pet or as a show dog.

The Irish Terrier is active, lively, and behaves with cocky self-assurance. The head is long and fairly narrow; the eyes are dark and fiery. The tail is docked slightly longer than in most other terriers and is carried erect, not over the back. The coat is wiry, close, and not so long as to hide the outline of the body.

The Irish Terrier is whole-colored, the most desirable color being shades of red.

The height at the shoulder is about 18 inches, with the weight around 26 pounds.

Irish Water Spaniel *Britain*

The more one looks at an Irish Water Spaniel, the harder it is to believe that it is a true spaniel. Not only is it much larger than the other varieties, it is also completely different in shape and general characteristics. In many ways it resembles the Poodle, a breed which must figure among its ancestors.

In fact the Irish Water Spaniel has evolved from several different types of spaniel common in Ireland and Scotland toward the end of the nineteenth century. Although it was recognized as a breed earlier than most other gundogs, in Britain it has remained fairly rare. It is a sturdily built dog, eager and intelligent. The eyes are small, brown, bright, and alert; the ears very long, low-set, and covered with twisted curls. The coat is an important characteristic: it has a natural oiliness and is composed of dense, tight ringlets – profuse everywhere except on the muzzle, just above the eyes, and on the tail where the ringlets stop abruptly a few inches below the root.

The color is always a dark liver with a purplish tint. The height at the shoulder for dogs is about 21 to 23 inches, 20 to 22 inches for bitches.

Below left: Irish Terrier.
Below: Irish Water Spaniel.

Irish Wolfhound *Eire*

The Irish Wolfhound is one of the tallest dogs in the world, and the breed is also one of the oldest. For centuries Irish Wolfhounds were used by the Irish Celts for hunting, and they were famous throughout the Western world. (In AD 393 a Roman senator wrote to his brother stationed in Britain thanking him for a gift of seven Irish hounds. 'All Rome viewed them with wonder,' he said. This was hardly surprising since they stood well over 3 feet at the shoulder and weighed 150 pounds apiece.)

With its great size, impressive bulk, and rough gray coat, it would seem that the Wolfhound has everything needed to make it the ideal, awe-inspiring guard. Its threatening presence, however, is softened by its gentle, dark eyes and an affectionate, friendly disposition. As a companion and pet the Wolfhound is docile and manageable and, partly because of these attributes, needs less space than one would imagine.

The Irish Wolfhound is muscular and strongly, though gracefully, built. The coat is rough and especially long on the head. The color is usually a shade of gray, but may be black, white, fawn, red, or brindle. The minimum height for dogs is 31 inches (32 inches for the USA), weight 120 pounds; bitches 28 inches and 90 pounds (30 inches and 105 pounds for the USA).

Istrski Kratkodlaki Gonic, Istrski Resati Gonic *Yugoslavia*

The Istrski Gonic hounds are Istrian sporting dogs resembling in appearance the British Pointer. The smooth-haired Kratkodlaki is the more common variety; the Resati shares most of the characteristics of its smooth-haired relative – with the exception of the coat.

The color, according to the breed standard, is 'snow white with orange markings on the ears.' The height at the shoulder for dogs varies between 18 and 23 inches, while bitches should not exceed 21 inches. The average weight is about 40 pounds.

Italian Greyhound *Italy*

The Italian Greyhound, the Piccolo Levriero Italiano, is the smallest of the sight-hound breeds, but it belongs to the great Greyhound family (which includes the Irish Wolfhound, Scottish Deerhound, Saluki, and Afghan). Italian Greyhounds were originally bred from the smallest greyhounds, resulting in a miniature breed. For centuries this graceful and elegant miniature Greyhound has been a popular

Above: Italian Greyhound.
Right: Irish Wolfhound.

pet and has rarely been employed as a sight hound – although in medieval Europe it was occasionally used for rabbiting – and today Italian Greyhounds are raced in some countries. They are very gentle and affectionate by nature and make excellent house dogs.

In the show ring, great emphasis is placed on its elegance, fine bone, and high-stepping, graceful action. It is well proportioned and sound, without appearing dwarfish, and is not as delicate as it may appear. In many respects it resembles its larger cousins, the Whippet and the Greyhound, but it is not only smaller but more slender in all respects.

Desirable color and markings vary slightly from country to country; fawn, cream, or blue, however, are always acceptable. The size and weight, too, vary between countries. Generally a weight not exceeding 10 pounds and a height at the shoulder of between 13 and 15 inches are considered the most desirable.

Italian Sheepdog, see Maremma

Jack Russell Terrier *Britain*

Strictly speaking, the Jack Russell has no place in this catalog since it is not a recognized breed, and the Kennel Club insists that it is merely a 'type' of terrier. (To be recognized a breed must have a breed standard – a specification laying down physical requirements.)

Nevertheless, because these little dogs are so popular in Britain, they deserve a mention. In type they vary from one area to another, and today's Jack Russells probably look very different to those owned and hunted by the sporting Devonshire parson from whom they take their name. Some have medium-length legs, others have short ones; some have prick ears, others the drop variety; some are brown and white, others black and white; and coats vary from smooth, through shaggy to wiry. But they all are game, gay little dogs.

Jämthund *Sweden*

The Jämthund is a Swedish breed that has been officially recognized only since 1946. It was evolved for elk hunting and, although it is numerically one of the strongest breeds in Sweden, it is little known outside its home country.

The Jämthund is up to 4 inches taller than the Elkhound. The head is slightly longer than the Elkhound's with a very strong, less pointed foreface. The ears are pointed and very mobile, the eyes dark with a keen expression. The tail, which has no plume, is carried fairly loosely and curled over the back. The coat is thick and close to the body but longer on the chest, neck, buttocks, and tail.

The color is gray with cream markings on the muzzle, cheeks, throat, and under the body. The height at the shoulder is 23 to 25 inches for dogs, 21 to 23 inches for bitches.

Japanese Akita *Japan*

The Akita, sometimes known as the large or Shishi Inu, is the biggest and one of the best known of the Japanese breeds. It comes from the Polar regions and was bred for hunting deer and wild boar. In former times it could be owned only by Japanese nobility. Today it is gaining favor in the United States where there are several specialist Akita breeders. The Akita loves to work, but also makes a good, gentle pet.

The Akita is swift, and with its webbed feet is a powerful swimmer. Its double coat and soft mouth enable it to retrieve even in the coldest waters. The top coat is medium to soft and straight; the undercoat thick and furry. It is large, compact and muscular with a fairly short neck, straight back and sturdy straight legs. The tail is curled and carried over the back. Colors are fawn, wheaten gray, brindle, russet, tan or black and tan, and all white. The height at the shoulder is 21 to 24 inches for dogs, and 19 to 21 inches for bitches.

Japanese Spaniel (or Japanese Chin) *Japan*

The Japanese Spaniel and the Pekingese have a great deal in common and it is thought that they share a common oriental ancestry. The Japanese Spaniel has, however, longer legs than the Pekingese, a lighter body, and moves more gracefully. For centuries this dainty and elegant 'toy' dog graced the homes of Japanese nobles, and it was not until well after Commodore Perry had opened Japan to the West that they came to the United States and Europe. Japanese Spaniels first appeared in Britain about 1880, and Queen Alexandra had several.

They make delightful and handsome pets. The head is fairly large and rounded with a flat nose and a slight 'wrinkle' on the upper lip. The eyes are large and dark with the whites clearly showing at the inner corners. The coat is profuse and long, free from curl, and particularly abundant on the tail, thighs, front legs, and feet.

The color is always white with evenly distributed patches in black or a shade of red. Size varies and, though the smaller the better, it may have a height at shoulder of up to 11 inches.

Right: Jack Russell Terrier.
Below: Japanese Chin.

Japanese Spitz *Japan*

The Japanese Spitz is a Japanese version of the Pomeranian – cream or white in color – slightly larger than its British relative. This breed is a comparatively recent development. Outside Japan it is not known.

Japanese Terrier *Japan*

The Japanese Terrier is descended from British terrier breeds – mainly the Smooth Fox Terrier – but, in the course of its evolution, the breed has lost many of its terrier characteristics.

The Japanese Terrier is described as a 'streamlined' Fox Terrier with a sparse, smooth coat. The color is usually white with smaller markings in black and tan. It is slightly taller than the British Fox Terrier.

Karelian Bear Dog *Finland*

This breed, the Karjalankarhukoira, belongs to the great spitz family of dogs. It takes its name from the Karelia region of Finland (now the Karelo–Finnish Socialist Republic), and is clearly related to the Russo–Finnish Laika. In Finland the Karelian Bear Dog was recognized as a pure breed in 1935, and the Fédération Cynologique Internationale officially recognized it in 1946.

These dogs have an excellent nose and are used to hunt bear and elk. They are said to be bold and intelligent, but also intensely stubborn and individualistic. The head is typical of the spitz breeds with erect ears and dark, alert eyes. The tail is curled, preferably not bobbed or short. The coat is straight and coarse, hanging loosely away from the body.

The color is black shading into brown, often with white markings on the head, neck, abdomen, legs, and tip of the tail. The height at the shoulder is 21 to 24 inches for dogs, 19 to 21 inches for bitches.

Keeshond *Holland*

The Keeshond (pronounced 'kayshond') is named after a celebrated eighteenth-century Dutch patriot, who owned one of the spitz-type dogs which were the predecessors of the modern Keeshond. For centuries these dogs were used as guard dogs and as barge dogs on the Dutch canals. In the early 1920s a Miss Hamilton Fletcher took some of these barge dogs back to England and bred from them, and the Dutch Barge Dog, as it was then known, became very popular in the United Kingdom. Keeshonds thrive on companionship and are dependable pets.

The Keeshond is short and compact with a bold expression. A unique feature of the breed is the so-called 'spectacles,' that is, lighter shadings round the dark, almond-shaped eyes. The ears are small and erect, the body deep and sturdy, and the tail tightly curled, even with a double curl, over the back. The coat is thick and straight, hanging loosely from the body, and is particularly abundant around the neck, where it forms a large ruff, and on the buttocks.

The color is all gray with dark tips. The height at the shoulder is about 18 inches for dogs, 17 inches for bitches.

Right: Keeshond.
Below: Japanese Spitz.

Kelpie *Australia*

The Kelpie, or 'barb' as it is sometimes called, is the Australian sheepdog, descended from short-haired, prick-eared Scottish sheepdogs which were sent to Australia about 1870. It is considered to have exceptional qualities of scent, sight, and hearing, and plays a key role on Australia's vast sheep-rearing stations, rounding up sheep that have strayed from the flock. One well-trained Kelpie, it is said, can do the work of six men.

The Kelpie is a clean-cut, tough, and muscular dog with a fox-like head. The stop is well defined; the eyes are almond-shaped and may be light or dark according to the color of the coat. The ears are set wide apart and carried erect at a slight angle. The neck is clearly arched. The body is lithe, the back of moderate length giving a rectangular outline. It is not too heavy in bone, the feet are well knuckled up with hard pads and strong nails. The tail is bushy and is carried low in repose or high in action. The coat is short, straight, thick, and feels rough to the touch.

The color may be black, black and tan, red, red and tan, fawn, chocolate, or smoke blue. Dogs stand about 18 to 20 inches at the shoulder.

Kerry Blue Terrier *Eire*

The Kerry Blue Terrier (sometimes known as the Irish Blue Terrier) has its background deep in the remoteness of southwest Ireland, and a number of legends are associated with its ancestry. It has been said that Kerry Blues have Irish Wolfhound blood in them, but more likely is the simple fact that dogs of the Kerry Blue type are indigenous to Ireland. However, the blue color must have been intensified by selected breeding, and it has also been suggested that the color and coat texture were enhanced by the introduction of Bedlington Terriers. Whatever the background, it has since 1920 become popular in both Britain and the United States, and is gaining popularity in the Netherlands and Germany.

In size the Kerry Blue stands midway between the Airedale and the Bedlington. Puppies and young dogs are always black and all too frequently the desired blue color never appears, even in fully grown animals. The height at the shoulder for dogs is 18 to 19 inches, slightly less for bitches. The ideal weight is about 35 pounds.

King Charles Spaniel *Britain*

The King Charles Spaniel was at one time more popular and more common than its close relative, the Cavalier King Charles Spaniel. Nowadays the position is reversed. The basic difference between the two breeds is that the King Charles has a flatter nose than the Cavalier and is frequently smaller.

There are four color varieties: black and tan, Blenheim (white and chestnut), tricolor (white, black, and tan), and ruby (whole-colored rich red). The breed standard does not specify height. The desirable weight is 6 to 12 pounds.

Right: King Charles Spaniel.
Below: Kerry Blue Terrier.

Komondor *Hungary*

The Komondor is the largest of the Hungarian dogs used for guarding flocks of sheep and herds of cattle. It is of Asian origin and is probably related to Russian herding dogs. The Komondor has a long and profuse coat (which by tradition in Hungary is never groomed). This coat, which consists of either flat or round 'cords,' protects it as effectively from the heat in summer as from the cold in winter. The Komondor has also proved to be an excellent pet and has become quite popular as a show dog, notably in the United States. They make very good watchdogs.

The color is always white. The height for dogs ranges from 26 to 32 inches.

Krasky Ovcar *Yugoslavia*

The Krasky Ovcar is a Yugoslavian sheepdog, similar in appearance to the Leonberger but smaller and lighter. It has a thick profuse coat, and the color is iron gray. The ideal height at the shoulder for dogs is 23 inches, 21 inches for bitches.

Kromfohrländer *Germany*

This breed, still quite rare, is a hunting dog, which is reportedly used today as a hunting terrier in some parts of Europe. It originates from crosses between Wirehaired Fox Terriers and a Griffon breed from Brittany.

The Kromfohrländer has a flat, wedge-shaped skull, hardly any stop, and a powerful, fairly broad foreface. The ears are set high and vee-shaped. The back is straight and broad with a deep chest. The tail is set high and carried curled to the left side of the back. The coat is short but coarse.

The color is white with brown patches. The height at the shoulder is 15 to 18 inches.

Kuvasz *Hungary*

The Kuvasz is an old breed whose ancestors are believed to have been taken to Hungary by the Kurds about AD 1100. Its name is a corruption of the Turkish word *kawasz*, which means 'guardian of the peace.' Originally a sheepdog – a guardian of the flocks – the breed was also used to hunt wild boar. Nowadays they have reverted to their original guard-dog role, but their watchfulness, size, and great strength plus friendly temperament have also made them popular as household companions. The similarity between the Kuvasz and Pyrenean Mountain Dog suggests that they are closely related.

A typical Kuvasz is tall and powerful, and moves in a slow, dignified manner. The shape of the head is very important; it is noble and expressive and the foreface is neither sharp nor coarse. The eyes are dark brown with a fierce expression. The tail is carried low except when the dog is alert, in which case it may be slightly raised; the tip of the tail is often hooked. The coat is short on the head, ears, and feet but long, wavy, and fairly coarse, especially around the neck, on the tail, and on the back of the legs.

The color is pure white, but ivory shades are acceptable. The height at the shoulder is 28 to 30 inches for dogs, and 26 to 27 inches for bitches.

Kyushu Nippon Inu, Shika *Japan*

This is one of the medium-sized Japanese spitz breeds, originally used for hunting deer but kept nowadays mainly as a companion and guard dog. It is rarely found outside Japan.

The color of the Kyushu may be shades of pepper and salt, red, black, or white. The height at the shoulder for dogs is 19 to 21 inches, 17 to 19 inches for bitches.

Kuvasz (above) and Komondor (right).

Labrador Retriever *Britain*

The aristocratic but powerfully built Labrador Retriever is a true British breed, despite its name. Some of its ancestors, however, were Newfoundland dogs taken to Britain by Canadian fishermen who sailed there to sell their catches. Subsequently the breed was developed by crossbreeding in order to produce gundogs, and in 1903 it was recognized by the Kennel Club of Britain. Since then it has gained great popularity both as a working dog and as a pet.

The general appearance of the Labrador is that of a strongly built, powerful dog. Its color is usually black or yellow, though some are liver and these may be lighter in eye and have a liver-colored nose. The height at the shoulder is about 22 inches for dogs, 21 to 22 inches for bitches.

Laekenois *Belgium*

The Laekenois, like its relative the Groenendael, is a Belgian sheepdog. (The other main varieties are the Malinois and Tervueren.) It is a coarse-haired animal with a

tousled appearance and characteristics similar to the Groenendael. The Lakenois' color is fawn with traces of black, mainly at the muzzle and tail. See also *Belgian Shepherd*.

Laika *USSR*

Most people in the West had never heard of the Laika until the Russians told the world that they had put a dog into space orbit; this dog, they announced, was called 'Laika.' In fact Laika (which comes from a word for 'barking') is the name given to five different varieties of a spitz-type breed found in the northern parts of the Soviet Union. None of them is especially common outside its home area where it is used as a guard dog or as a barking gundog, (and more recently for medical experiments – including those related to the Soviet space program).

The famous space dog Laika was probably one of the Russo-European variety of the breed. This is the medium-sized representative of the Laika family. It is sturdily built with dark, slightly obliquely

Below: Labrador Retrievers.

set eyes, a thick, rough coat, and a curled tail.

Its color is gray, fawn, or black and reddish gray. The height at the shoulder varies from about 20 to 25 inches.

The West Siberian Laika is about the same size as its Russo-European cousin, with a wedge-shaped head and triangular-shaped ears. Its color is usually white with orange patches.

The Karelian or Russo-Finnish Laika is the smallest member of the Laika family and it greatly resembles the Finnish Spitz. In the home area these dogs are used not only for hunting but for hauling sledges and herding cattle. The Karelian Laika is of square build with a leaner, more pointed head than the West Siberian and Russo-European varieties and has a tightly curled tail. The coat is thick and profuse and the color is a yellow-fawn. The height at the shoulder is generally between 16 and 19 inches.

Lakeland Terrier *Britain*

The Lakeland Terrier hails from the Lake District in Cumbria, the English Border country adjoining Scotland. It is in fact a comparatively recent breed, although its ancestors, like those of most other British terrier breeds, have been around for centuries.

The Lakeland Terrier was bred originally for work with Border farmers, plagued with foxes which preyed on the young sheep. The dogs they needed in the Lake District had to be killers, small enough to go after foxes which went to ground, agile enough to crawl long distances, and capable of walking or jogging from the kennels to the scene of operations. As with most British terriers, there was a fair amount of crossbreeding and the lively, hard-working, and fearless dog that finally emerged leaned more toward the Wire-haired Fox Terrier than is considered desirable by today's standard.

Nowadays the Lakeland Terrier may easily be mistaken for the Welsh Terrier, although it is more heavily built, usually has more coat on the head and the legs, and has a greater variety of colors. The head is well balanced with powerful jaws. The eyes are larger than the Fox Terrier's and the back only moderately short. The tail, as with most terriers, is set and carried high; the coat is rough.

The color varies from whole-colored wheaten to pure black. The height at the shoulder should not exceed just over 14 inches. The weight is usually about 16 pounds.

Below left: Lackenois.
Below: Lakeland Terrier.

Laplandic Herder *Finland*

The Laplandic Herder is a working dog used by the Laplanders to herd reindeer. In appearance it closely resembles the Swedish Lapphund, and stands about 19 to 22 inches high at the shoulder.

Lapphund *Sweden*

The original Lapphunds were probably used for hunting wild reindeer, but when the Laplanders domesticated their reindeer the Lapphunds were trained as herders.

The Lapphund is a fairly low-set dog, a little under medium size, and a typical spitz. Its coat is profuse and almost lank.

The most desirable color is considered to be dark brown but black is common. Brown and white, however, are also acceptable. The height at the shoulder for dogs is 18 to 20 inches, 16 to 18 inches for bitches.

Leonberger *Germany*

The Leonberger, a German breed, is rarely found outside its native country. It has been produced by crossing St Bernards with black and white Newfoundlands and Pyrenean Mountain Dogs.

The Leonberger has a broad head with a domed skull and marked stop. The ears, which are set high, are big, soft, and pendulous. The coat is thick and fairly long. The color is fawn, gray fawn, or orange, generally with darker markings around the muzzle and eyes. The minimum height for dogs at the shoulder is 30 inches, 28 inches for bitches.

Levesque *France*

The Levesque, a French hound, is a relatively new breed descended from a cross between a Griffon and a Foxhound, interbred with other varieties of hound. Its color is black and white; its coat is short; the tail is long, set high, and carried in a curve. The height at the shoulder is 26 to 28 inches for dogs, 25 to 27 inches for bitches.

Right: Leonberger.

Lhasa Apso *Tibet*

The Lhasa Apso – so-called in the United States and Canada but often called the Tibetan Apso in Britain – is a Tibetan toy breed. (Apso is the Tibetan word for goat – an animal to which the dog has some resemblance.) It is fairly rare in some countries and is often mistaken for the more common Shih Tzu. In fact the Apso is a true Tibetan dog, while the Shih Tzu is said to have originated in western China. However the two breeds undoubtedly mixed, since the Dalai Lama presented Apsos to high-ranking foreigners visiting Tibet and the Emperor of China gave Shih Tzus to dignitaries visiting Peking. Thus Apsos found their way to Peking and Shih Tzus to Lhasa.

The Lhasa or Tibetan Apso is 10 to 11 inches high at the shoulder. The weight is 8 to 15 pounds. The most common color is golden (other colors are sandy, honey, dark grizzle, slate, smoke, particolors, black, white or brown). The coat is heavy, straight, hard, and dense, of medium length and parted along the spine. The head is heavily covered with hair, with a fall over the eyes. The nose is black, the eyes dark, the ears pendant and heavily feathered.

Lion dogs

A number of breeds have been called 'lion' dogs. With the exception of the Rhodesian Ridgeback they have all been small dogs with a lion-like look about them. But the Rhodesian Ridgeback is the only breed with any real entitlement to the name, since they are heavy, strong dogs which come from lion country and which, in the past, have been used to hunt lions.

Other breeds dubbed lion dogs at one time or another have been the Pekingese, the Lhasa Apso, and the Löwchen (little lion) or Bichon Petit Chien Lion. Löwchens weigh about 12 pounds each and closely resemble the Poodle. They come in whole colors, white, cream, blue, and black and their coats are clipped, Poodle-fashion, to leave a lion's mane and tail tuft while the rest of the body is shaved clean.

Right: Lhasa Apso.
Below: Lion Dog.

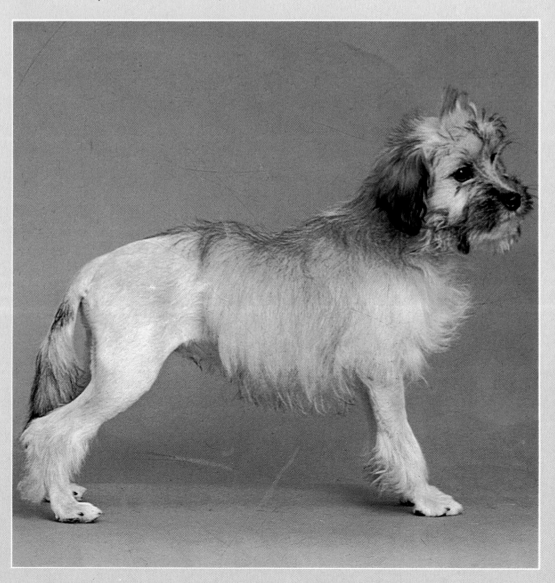

Löwchen, see **Lion dogs**

Above: Lucerne Laufhund.
Right: Maltese.

Lucerne Laufhund *Switzerland*
The Lucerne Laufhund is a Harrier/Fox-hound type similar to its close relative the Swiss Laufhund, but of lighter build. It is rarely found outside Switzerland.

Lurcher *Britain*
The Lurcher is a British dog type, not an official breed. The name is given to intelligent crossbred Greyhound/terrier animals, which have the reputation of being poachers' dogs.

Magyar Agár *Hungary*
The Magyar Agár is a Hungarian sight-hound. The breed obviously shares its ancestry with other sighthounds, but was kept from interbreeding with them for over a thousand years. However, in the nineteenth century blood was introduced from the British Greyhound.

The Magyar Agár is muscular, strongly built, with a well-defined body and a head which has a stop similar to that of the Greyhound. The coat is short and smooth, but often grows longer during the winter. The color varies but is usually black or brindle, sometimes particolored. The breed standard does not specify height, but the weight should be about 59 to 68 pounds for dogs, 48 to 57 pounds for bitches.

Mahratta, see **Eastern Greyhound**

Malamute, see **Alaskan Malamute**

Maltese *Italy*
The gay, good-natured little Maltese is the oldest toy breed in the West. It probably takes its name not from the island of Malta as one might expect, but from the Sicilian town of Melita. In any event there is evidence that the Maltese, or Canis Melitei, was established in the Mediterranean area at the time of the Roman Empire and it was a popular pet even then. It has changed little over the centuries and is still largely the same breed it was in ancient times.

Underneath its flowing coat, the Maltese has a rather low-set body. The luxuriant coat is the breed's most prominent feature: it is very long all over, straight and silky and nearly reaches the ground.

Pure white is the most desirable color, but all colors are acceptable – according to the Italian breed standard – as long as the dog is not particolored. In common with most toy breeds, the Maltese should be as small as possible. The weight should not exceed 8 pounds and the height at the shoulder should not be above 10 inches for both dogs and bitches.

Manchester Terrier *Britain*

This breed supposedly originated in Manchester as the result of mating what was described as an 'English' terrier with a Whippet. The aim was to produce a breed that would kill rats and catch rabbits.

In appearance the Manchester Terrier resembles the Smooth Fox Terrier, with which it has much in common. According to the breed standard it is a compact dog with good bone. The head is long and narrow, the eyes are small, set close, dark, and sparkling. The neck is long and slightly arched, the back moderately curved and the tail, which is carried low, is thick at the root and tapers to a point. The coat is smooth, short, and glossy.

The background color must be black with rich mahogany tan markings on muzzle, cheeks, above eyes, below knees, on each side of the chest, and on the vent. The height at shoulder is about 16 inches for dogs, 15 inches for bitches. The weight should not be more than 22 pounds.

Maremma *Italy*

The Maremma is *the* Italian sheepdog, but it is also a companionable pet. In Britain it has been known since 1931 but very few Maremmas have been taken across the Atlantic. Judging by its appearance the breed appears to have much in common with the Hungarian Kuvasz and the Pyrenean Mountain Dog.

The Italian breed standard calls for a dog which has a pure white coat with long, slightly wavy hair, a square-built and moderately broad skull with a medium stop, and a fairly long, tapered jaw. The eyes are dark brown, the nose black; the ears fold over to the sides of the head. The tail, which is heavily feathered, is carried low. The height at the shoulder should be 26 to 29 inches for dogs, and 24 to 27 inches for bitches. Dogs average about 75 pounds in weight.

Right: Maremma.
Below: Manchester Terrier.

Mastiff/Old English Mastiff *Britain*

Before pure-bred dogs were recognized as such, any large dog was often called a Mastiff. Today, only three breeds are classified as Mastiffs, of which the best known is the Old English Mastiff. The other two are the rare Tibetan Mastiff and the Japanese Tosa. (See also *Spanish Mastiff, Alpine Mastiff, Bullmastiff, Tibetan Mastiff.*)

The Old English Mastiff is a tall, powerful dog considerably bigger than its relative the Bullmastiff, but not as heavily built. Its nose is not as blunt although it is still broad and square; the eyes are small and dark. The Old English Mastiff has a greater reach of neck than the Bullmastiff and is considerably higher in the leg. The tail is fairly long; the coat is short and close. The color is usually apricot or fawn, with black on the muzzle and ears and around the eyes. Dogs stand about 30 inches at the shoulder, bitches $27\frac{1}{2}$ inches.

Mastin de los Pirineos *Spain*

This is the Pyrenean Mastiff, and it should not be confused with the internationally better-known Pyrenean Mountain Dog. Although the two breeds have some common features, the Mastin de los Pirineos – a huge and powerful dog with a broad and heavy head – is of distinct Mastiff type.

Its color is white with large patches of gray or fawn on the head and, occasionally, on the body. The height at the shoulder varies between 28 and 32 inches. The weight is 120 to 155 pounds.

Miniature Bull Terrier, see Bull Terrier

Miniature Pinscher *Germany*

Many people erroneously call the Zwerg-pinscher – the Miniature Pinscher – a Miniature Dobermann, or conversely call the Dobermann Pinscher a 'Standard' Dobermann. The Zwergpinscher and the Dobermann Pinscher do, in fact, bear a striking resemblance to each other, but the Zwergpinscher is a much older breed. It is a tiny, elegant, and lively little dog and one of the most popular toy breeds in the world. Characteristics are a narrow, wedge-shaped head, a square body with a deep chest, dark brown and piercing black eyes, and a black nose (except with chocolate-colored Pinschers, when it may be brown). The coat should be short and glossy.

The color should be red or lustrous black with tan markings. The ideal height at the shoulder should not exceed 12 inches and the weight is about 6 to 8 pounds.

Above right: Miniature Pinschers.
Right: Old English Mastiff.

Mongrel

In a straightforward catalog of breeds, 'mongrel' has no place, for it is the name given to dogs of mixed breeds. Whether or not the parents are of mixed breed or purebreds of different breeds, the progeny of such unions will be mongrels. Unscrupulous breeders have in recent years crossed Cocker Spaniels and Poodles or Pekingese and Poodles and advertised the offspring as Cockapoos or Pekapoos. The fact remains that they are simply mongrels.

Having said this, it is fair to add that mongrels also have a place in the canine world. Many of them are remarkably intelligent and serve as lovable pets.

Moth, see Phalène

Mudi *Hungary*

The Mudi is a Hungarian herding breed which is also used as a guard dog. It is slightly longer than its height at the shoulder, and has a long head with a pointed muzzle and hardly any stop. The ears are vee-shaped, pointed, and erect, the eyes oval, dark, and slightly obliquely set. The tail is short and is usually carried hanging down. The color is either black or white, occasionally a combination of the two, in small, even spots. The height at the shoulder is 14 to 19 inches.

Münchener Dog, see Schnauzer

Münsterländer *Germany*

There are two distinct but closely related breeds of Münsterländer – the Kleiner (small) and the Grosser (large) Münster-länder. The small breed, which is between a Cocker Spaniel and a Setter in appearance, is by far the more common. It is used as a retriever and as a pointing gundog. Outside Germany it is not commonly found.

The color of the Kleiner Münster-länder is usually liver roan and white with larger liver-colored patches. The height at the shoulder is 20 to 22 inches for dogs, 19 to 21 inches for bitches.

The Grosser Münsterländer is virtually a larger version of its smaller relative. Its color, however, is usually white with black markings – either large patches or a mass of small 'freckles,' commonly called roan. The height at the shoulder is 23 to 25 inches.

Neapolitan Mastiff *Italy*

The Mastino Napoletano is the Italian Mastiff, said to be the descendant of the war dogs of ancient Rome. Today, it is employed as a guard dog by the Italian police and armed forces. Like its British counterpart, the Neapolitan Mastiff is one of the largest and heaviest breeds. It has an enormous head with lots of loose skin. In Italy its ears are always cropped short, and the eye color matches or is darker than the coat color. The tail is saber-shaped and is not carried over the back.

Acceptable colors are black, gray, and brindle, occasionally with small white spots on the chest and toes. The height at the shoulder may be up to 30 inches, but averages between 26 and 28 inches for dogs, 24 and 27 inches for bitches. The weight varies between 110 and 154 pounds.

Right: A mongrel. Below: Neapolitan Mastiff.

Newfoundland *Newfoundland*

There is much uncertainty about the origin of the massive Newfoundland dog. One American canine authority has claimed that it is descended from Pyrenean Mountain Dogs (Great Pyrenees) taken to Newfoundland in the middle of the seventeenth century by Basque fishermen. Other authorities believe that the Husky and other breeds may be counted among its ancestors. In any event the dog that evolved in the Newfoundland environment was particularly suited to the island.

He was a big strong dog, with a heavy coat to protect him from the long winters and icy waters. His feet were large, strong, and webbed, enabling him to traverse marshland and the Newfoundland coastal terrain. Apart from his physical powers he also developed an attractive disposition and it was primarily this that led to his being taken to England where he was extensively bred. In consequence today most pedigreed Newfoundlands – even in Newfoundland – are descended from forbears which were born in the United Kingdom.

The breed standard of the Newfoundland reflects the fact that it is essentially a working dog – and one that is as much at home in the water as on dry land. In its native land the Newfoundland is still used to drag carts or as a pack animal; in the past such dogs have been employed to help their fishermen owners with their heavy nets. To perform these duties the Newfoundland must be a big dog with powerful hind-quarters and a lung capacity enabling him to swim for great distances.

His head is massive, has a distinct stop, and is free of wrinkles. The muzzle is square and deep; the eyes are small and brown and deep-set; ears, which are small and triangular with rounded tips, lie close to the head. The length of the dog's body from withers to base of tail is approximately equal to its height, though bitches may be slightly longer than tall. The large cat-like feet are completely webbed. The tail is broad, well furred, and reaches to below the hocks.

The Newfoundland has a water-resistant double coat, the outer coat being moderately long and full but straight and flat. The color is generally a dull black, but there may be a tinge of bronze or a splash of white on the toes or chest. Male Newfoundland dogs average 28 inches at the shoulder and weigh about 150 pounds. Bitches are slightly smaller.

Niederlaufhund *Switzerland*

The Niederlaufhund is a short-legged Foxhound, and there are four varieties of it – known by regional names (Berner, Jura, Luzerner, and Schweizer) – which differ only in color. It is related to the Swiss Laufhund but looks longer, lighter, and leaner. The height at the shoulder is only about 12 to 15 inches.

Above: Luzerner Niederlaufhund.
Right: Newfoundland.

Norfolk Terrier *Britain*
The Norfolk Terrier was recognized as a separate breed by the British Kennel Club only comparatively recently. Until then it was regarded as a variety of Norwich Terrier. In effect the Norfolk differs from the Norwich in only a few minor points.

Norwegian Buhund *Norway*
Travellers to Norway may see little Norwegian Buhunds outside remote mountain huts or farms, where they act as watchdogs or general purpose farm dogs. The breed was first exported to England in 1946 and in 1968 the Norwegian Buhund Club was recognized by the British Kennel Club. Buhunds have also been exported to Australia where they have become very popular as working dogs. They are in fact ideal family dogs, being gay, lively, and very friendly. They are natural herders, rounding up anything from cattle to poultry, but are also excellent companions for children.

The standard for a Norwegian Buhund calls for a fearless, brave and energetic animal: a typical spitz dog of under middle size, lightly built with short compact body, erect pointed ears, with a tail carried curled over the back. The coat should be close and harsh with soft wool undercoat, the eyes a lively dark brown, the ears very mobile.

A large range of colors is permissible – all shades of wheaten, red, wolf-sable and black – but in Norway the lighter shades of wheaten are preferred. The height for dogs is about 18 inches; bitches are slightly smaller.

Norwegian Elkhound *Norway*
The Norwegian Elkhound – often known more simply as the Elkhound or Elk – is a working dog and a typical spitz breed. The

sharp comparatively small but erect ears, the straight hocks, the ruff around the neck and the tail tightly curled over the back are all clear indicators of its origin. In effect its home and its task are given by its name. It was, and still is, used to hunt moose in Scandinavia in general and in Norway in particular. The Elkhound is a large ungainly animal. As a hunter, however, he has the courage, agility, and stamina to hold big game at bay by barking and dodging attack, and the endurance to track for long hours in all weather over rough terrain. In temperament the elk is bold and energetic – an effective guard dog, yet normally friendly but independant in character.

In appearance the Elkhound is a typical northern dog of medium size and substance, with a compact short body, thick coat, and tail tightly curled over the center line of the back. The head is broad between the prick ears, muzzle broad at base, tapering gradu-

ally but not pointed. The stop is not large yet clearly defined. The eyes are very dark brown, medium in size, oval, not protruding. Ears are set high, firm and erect, pointed and with their height slightly greater than their width at base. The neck is of medium length, firm, and muscular. The body is square in profile with a wide straight back; the chest is broad and deep. The loins are muscular and the feet compact with small, slightly oval, paws. The coat should be thick, hard, abundant, weather-resistant, and smooth lying. The color is generally a medium gray with black tips on the outer coat, a lighter shade on the chest, stomach, and underside of the tail. The weight is approximately 55 pounds for dogs and 48 pounds for bitches. The height at the shoulder is 18 to 20½ inches.

Far left: Norwegian Buhund.
Below center: Norfolk Terrier.
Below: Norwegian Elkhound.

Norwich Terrier *Britain*

The Norwich Terrier is one of the smallest of the terriers, but it is said to be a 'demon' for its size. The breed was created by crossing the Irish Terrier with various short-legged terrier varieties and, like most British terriers, it takes its name from its place of origin.

The Norwich Terrier is a small, low, keen dog, compact and strong. It has a gay and fearless temperament and a lovable disposition. The head is not very long and has a well-defined stop; the skull is wide and slightly rounded. The eyes are dark, full of expression, bright, and keen; the ears can be erect or dropped. The tail is docked.

The color is red, red wheaten, black and tan, or grizzle. The height at the shoulder is about 10 inches.

Ogar Polski *Poland*

The Ogar Polski is a Harrier/Foxhound breed, little known outside Poland.

It is considerably heavier in build than mid-European and Scandinavian breeds. It has a powerful head with dark, slightly obliquely set eyes and fairly low-set ears. The tail is long and thick and, in action, carried in line with the back. The color is black, dark gray, or dark brown on the body, with other parts in a slightly lighter shade of brown. The height at the shoulder is 22 to 26 inches for dogs, 22 to 24 inches for bitches.

Old Danish Hönsehund *Denmark*

The Danes have evolved their own breed of gundog, the Gammel Dansk Hönsehund. The breed is now about 200 years old and it is said to have originated with crosses of gypsy and local farm dogs, with a dash of Bloodhound.

One of the most distinctive points of the breed is the marked difference between the dog and bitch: the dog is impressively heavy and massive, while the bitch is considerably lighter and more active. The head is fairly large and broad with a prominent occiput, the eyes – like the Bloodhound's – sometimes slightly red rimmed, the ears long and pendulous. Abundant folds of skin on the neck is one of the characteristics of the breed. The back slopes gradually toward the tail, which is carried high when the dog is in action. The coat is short and close.

The color is white with brown patches. Dogs stand 20 to 23 inches at the shoulder, bitches 19 to 21 inches.

Old English Sheepdog *Britain*

Although it is called 'old,' the Old English Sheepdog, the 'Bobtail' as it is sometimes called, is no more than 200 years old. Developed originally as a working dog to protect herds of cattle from beasts of prey, it has in recent years become a pet and companion. (The name 'Bobtail' stems from the practice of docking the tail – a custom associated with the breed's early days, when drovers' dogs were exempted from taxes and to prove their occupation were docked.) The Old English Sheepdog is similar to sheepdogs in the USSR, Italy, and the Pyrenees – massively built, with an abundance of coat all over. It stands slightly higher at the loins than at the shoulder and this gives it a characteristic rolling gait. The coat is not only profuse but shaggy and of good, strong texture.

The color is usually gray, grizzle, or blue with or without white markings. The height at the shoulder for dogs is about 22 inches; bitches are slightly smaller.

Right: Old English Sheepdog.
Below: Norwich Terrier.

Osterreichischer Bracke, Brandlbracke *Austria*

The Austrian Brandlbracke (literally flame-colored hound) is almost unknown outside its country of origin. It is a breed of setter, deriving its name from flame-colored markings on a black coat (although the color may also be wholly red). The Brandlbracke has a long head with brown, expressive eyes, a smooth and glossy coat, and a long tail. The height at the shoulder is usually about 20 inches.

Osterreichischer Kurzhaariger Pinscher *Austria*

This is the Austrian Short-haired Pinscher, which is little known outside Austria. The breed has not yet settled down to an agreed standard, insofar as the dogs can vary in size; ears may be dropped, erect, or semi-erect; and the tail may be either docked or carried over the back. The color is usually fawn, golden, red, or black and tan, often with 'brindle' markings. White markings on the muzzle, neck, chest, and feet are quite common. The height varies between 13 and 19 inches.

Otter Hound *Britain*

The Otter Hound has been known in Britain since the fourteenth century. It has a remarkable scenting ability, and is used for otter hunting. It is a big, courageous dog thoroughly at home in water, but it has an ungainly body, a large head, and webbed feet. The ears are long, thin, and pendulous; the neck is moderately short and looks practically nonexistent because of the abundant ruff around it. The tail is carried upward but not curled and, like the rest of the dog, is covered with a crisp and oily coat, which should not be soft and woolly.

The color is usually a sandy fawn or grizzle with more or less diffuse black and tan markings. The shoulder height is about 24 to 26 inches; weight is about 65 pounds.

Owcharka *USSR*

All the Russian sheepdogs are known as Owcharka, and there are at least four different varieties. Each is descended from the spitz breeds, crossed with other breeds to evolve herding dogs suited to local conditions. In the Caucasus, for example, where a dog was needed to protect the herds against wolves, the original spitz-type dog was crossed with the Mastiff, resulting in a heavy, powerful dog with a thick, warm coat. Other varieties are slightly smaller, usually not as heavily built and, except for the long-coated variety in the south of Russia, not as thickly coated as

Right: Papillons. Far right: Otter Hound.

the Caucasian variety.

The color varies: the Caucasian Owcharka is usually gray fawn but may also be white or even particolored. The height at the shoulder is about 26 inches.

Owczarek Podhalanski *Poland*

This is the oldest and largest of the two Polish herding breeds – said to be extremely courageous, loyal to its master, but fiercely antagonistic to others.

The Owczarek Podhalanski has dark eyes and an intelligent, lively expression. The ears are as wide at the base as they are long; the tail is long with a slight curve at the end. The feet are large and oval with very strong, hard pads. The coat is short and close on the head and foreface, but longer and very thick on other parts of the body, especially on the neck and rib cage. The coat is straight or slightly wavy.

The color is usually all white, sometimes pale cream. The minimum height at the shoulder for dogs is 26 inches.

Owczarek Polski Nizinny *Poland*

The Owczarek Polski Nizinny is the second – and smaller – of the two Polish herding breeds. It resembles the Old English Sheepdog, although its distant ancestry is more likely to be associated with the Tibetan Terrier. Like the Owczarek Podhalanski, it is employed as a sheepdog but it is easy to train and is popular as a pet in urban areas. The profuse, long coat may be straight or slightly wavy.

All colors and color combinations are acceptable, but blacks with white markings predominate. The height at the shoulder for dogs varies between 17 and 21 inches.

Papillon *France*

The Papillon derives its name from the fact that its ears, properly carried, should suggest an open-winged butterfly. It is a daintily balanced little toy dog with an attractive head, an alert bearing, and an intelligent and lively expression.

The Papillon was a great favorite of the aristocratic ladies of the French court prior to the French Revolution. Since 1793, more Papillons have been bred in Belgium and Britain than France, but it is claimed that the quality is equally high. The Papillon should be small and elegant, and the coat long and silky, forming profuse frills on the neck, chest, and thighs. The ears should be heavily fringed; the colour white with black and/or red markings. The weight should be about 4 pounds and the height at the shoulder should not exceed 12 inches.

Pariah dogs *Turkey and Southeast Asia*

Like the ubiquitous mongrel, the Pariah dog may be considered an outcast in this catalog of breeds, just as it is regarded as an outcast in its habitat. Pariahs are domestic dogs – or the descendants of domestic dogs – that have gone wild. They tend to congregate and forage for food around human settlements, and they can be tamed and trained to act as guard dogs. Pariahs come in a wide range of colors and sizes, and it has been argued that some purebreds such as the Israeli Canaan Dog have been evolved from Pariah stock.

Pastore Bergamasco *Italy*

The Pastore Bergamasco is an Italian herder, whose ancestors include the French Briard to which it bears some resemblance. It is a squarely built dog with a thick, luxuriant, long and curly coat. The ears are soft and pendulous; the eyes large and expressive. The color ranges from off-white to near black. The ideal height at shoulder is 24 inches for dogs and 22 inches for bitches, with an allowance of an inch or so either way. The weight is 70 to 84 pounds and 57 to 70 pounds respectively.

Pekingese *China*

The Pekingese has supposedly existed for 2000 years or more as the miniature dog of ancient China. It is certainly known that miniature dogs were kept as pets at the Imperial Court some 1500 years ago, but whether such dogs had the short faces, long coat, and large, flat feet of today's Pekes is open to doubt. In 1860, when the Summer Palace in Peking was sacked by British and French troops, five of the dogs belonging to the Chinese Emperor's aunt were found guarding the body. All five were taken back to England, and one was presented to Queen Victoria, two were given to the Duchess of Wellington, and two to the Duchess of Richmond. (Looty, Queen Victoria's dog, lived until she was 12 and was painted by several artists, including Landseer.) These dogs, mated with a few more Pekingese obtained by less adventurous methods, subsequently formed the basis of the present modern breed. The romantic story of Looty and her colleagues and the royal association made the Pekingese universely popular and demand for them was enormous. In any event, their individuality was enough to take the 'Pekes' to the top and it is certainly enough to keep them there. In Britain they have never been out of the top 20 breeds, and it seems they are as firmly placed there now as they were at the turn of the century.

The Pekingese is a small, well-balanced, bold, and dignified dog. He carries himself fearlessly with an alert and intelligent expression. His head is broad and he has large, lustrous eyes and a flat profile. The forequarters are thick-set and heavily boned with slightly bowed front legs, while the hindquarters are lighter and straight. The tail has a magnificent plume and is curved over the back. The coat is also particularly profuse on the neck, chest, thighs, and at the back of the front legs.

All colors except liver are acceptable. The height at the shoulder is 6 to 10 inches and the weight is 7 to 11 pounds for dogs, 8 to 12 pounds for bitches. Particularly small animals – so-called 'sleeve-dogs' because they were carried in the wide sleeves of the Chinese – still appear in litters of puppies of otherwise normal size.

Right: Pekingese.
Below: Pastore Bergamasco.

Perdiguero de Burgos *Spain*
The Perdiguero de Burgos is a pointer, and is rarely seen outside its native country. In Spain, however, it has for centuries enjoyed the reputation of being a first-class gundog.

The Perdiguero de Burgos is neither as agile nor as elegant as the English Pointer, not being as square in the body and having a long back, a large head with domed skull, a 'double chin,' and high-set, long, pendulous ears. The tail is docked to one-third of its natural length. The coat is smooth and short.

There are two color varieties: when white is the basic color, it should be marked with liver-colored spots of varying sizes; on a liver-colored dog, the coat should be mottled with white. The height at the shoulder for dogs should be between 26 to 30 inches.

Perdiguero Portugués *Portugal*
This Portuguese gundog is probably related to the Spanish Perdiguero de Burgos, and its forebears may have included the Italian Bracco. It is lighter than its Spanish relative, with a fairly broad head, short, blunt muzzle, thin, drooping ears, and a tail which is normally docked to a third of its natural length. The coat is short and coarse and colored golden brown. The height at the shoulder is about 22 inches for dogs.

Perro de Pastor Catalan *Spain*
This is a Spanish herding breed. In appearance it closely resembles the Bearded Collie, except that the Spanish dog has amber-colored eyes and its tail may be either long or short. Its coat is long and wavy; color a mixture of black and white with cream-colored legs and feet.

The height at the shoulder for dogs is 18 to 20 inches. The average weight is 40 pounds for dogs, 35 pounds for bitches.

Perro de Presa Malloquin *Spain*
The Perro de Presa Malloquin is a Spanish Bulldog, and in the Balearic Islands (from where it hails) it is employed as a guard dog. It has the typical broad and heavy head of the Bulldog with the small, thin 'rose' ears and a wide, low-slung chest. It is, however, longer in the neck than the British type and the tail is long and carried in a slight curve. The coat is short, brindle, and without white markings.

The height at the shoulder is about 23 inches.

Persian Greyhound, see **Afghan Hound** and **Saluki**

Phalène *France*
But for its ears, the French Phalène (literally 'moth') might be mistaken for a Papillon. (It is, in fact, an older breed than the Papillon, which only acquired its butterfly ears after the French Revolution when the Papillon was exiled to Belgium and crossed there with spitz breeds with erect ears.) The drop ears of the Phalène are a relic of its spaniel ancestors. However, apart from the ears, the breed is identical with the Papillon.

Pharaoh Hound *Egypt*
The Pharaoh Hound belongs to the Greyhound family and bears a very strong resemblance to the hound with large, erect ears depicted in ancient Egyptian sculptures.

A medium-sized dog in build, it is very like the modern Ibizan Hound. It is noted for its clean-cut, graceful lines, its reach, and large, erect ears. The tail should be set fairly high and carried above the level of the back. The eyes are amber or dark brown and the coat short, glossy, and smooth.

The basic color is often white with patches of gray or red; predominantly red specimens are, however, most common. The height at the shoulder for dogs is 25 to 28 inches.

Pinscher *Germany*
Reference to the 'Pinscher' has already been made under Dobermann Pinscher. There is, in fact, a medium-sized Pinscher – smaller than the standard Dobermann – and a Miniature Pinscher (Zwergpinscher). The Miniature is the more common. As may be expected, both bear strong resemblance to the Dobermann. Dogs of both breeds are clean-cut, elegant, and agile, with narrow, wedge-shaped heads and dark and sparkling eyes. The tail is set high and docked short, the coat short, smooth, hard, and glossy.

The color is usually black with small tan markings. The height at the shoulder for the 'medium' Pinscher is 16 to 19 inches, and for the Miniature it should not exceed 12 inches.

Plotthound *USA*
The Plotthound, a Coonhound, is not officially recognized as a breed by the American Kennel Club or in Britain, where it is virtually unknown. It may be described as a cross between the American Foxhound and the Black and Tan Coonhound.

Right: Pharaoh Hound.

Podengo Português *Portugal*

There are three varieties of Podengo Português – large, medium, and toy. The breed is used primarily for rabbiting and the largest of the three varieties is used to course hare. The largest variety has a conformation similar to that of the Ibizan Hound; the smallest has an affinity with the Chihuahua.

The Podengo has a pointed foreface, well-defined stop, and large, erect, and mobile ears. The tail is of medium length, thick, and is often carried absolutely straight up or slightly over the back. The coat may be smooth or wire-haired. The most common color is fawn. The height at the shoulder, for the largest Podengo variety, is 22 to 28 inches, 16 to 22 inches for the medium-sized variety, and 8 to 12 inches for the toy.

Pointer *Britain*

The name of this breed needs little or no explanation. The Pointer is a gundog which searches for game and, having found it, freezes and points with its nose. It is a beautiful and elegant animal, and in Britain it is now as popular as a show dog as it is in the field, where the land available for shooting has shrunk and so diminished the demand for such sporting dogs.

The hallmarks of the Pointer are a clean outline and elegance in appearance and movement. The skull should be of medium breadth and in proportion to the length of the face; the stop should be well pronounced and the muzzle slightly concave. The eyes should be either hazel or brown according to the color of the coat. The ears, which are fairly large, should lie close to the head. The neck should be long and arched, with the back sloping away to well-angulated hindquarters. The tail should be thick at the root, growing gradually thinner to the point, and carried level with the back. The coat should be short, close, and shiny.

The color of the English Pointer is white with black, lemon, or liver markings, or black, liver, or lemon with or without white. Dogs stand about 24 inches at the shoulder.

Polish Sheepdog *Poland*

There are two varieties of Polish sheepdog, the Tatra Mountain Dog (*Owczarek Podhalanski*) and the Lowlands Shepherd Dog (*Owczarek Nizinny*). Both are strong, vigilant guards and sheep herders, requiring very little in the way of care and sustenance. They are very resistant to extremes of weather.

The Tatra Mountain Dog is a large, docile, good-natured animal with a height of about 26 inches at the shoulder. It is rectangular in form. The head is well proportioned with a short muzzle and black nose. The ears, which are thick and triangular hang close to the cheek. The body is long and massive, back broad, and with straight powerful hindquarters. The coat is short on the head, long elsewhere – thick, straight or wavy. Color is creamy white.

The Lowlands Shepherd Dog is the livelier of the two breeds. Like the Tatra it is intelligent and docile, and it has an excellent memory. It is of medium size (16 to 20 inches high), and in appearance resembles the Old English sheepdog. All colors are permissible.

Pomeranian *Britain*

The Pomeranian is an attractive little dog, which evolved from German spitz breeds imported into Britain about a hundred years ago. The original Pomeranians were not especially popular; they had no sporting background, Britain had an ample supply of sheepdogs, and there was no call for them to pull carts as they did in Germany. However, interest was aroused by the occasional small puppies which were produced in otherwise 'normal' litters. These miniature 'Poms' normally weighed between 15 and 20 pounds and, when Queen Victoria showed an interest in them, their popularity soared. (Queen Victoria showed six Pomeranians in the 1891 Cruft's show, and when she died at Osborne in January 1901 her favorite black Pom lay at her feet on the end of the bed.) Over the next few years the breed was 'refined' by planned breeding, producing bigger coats, smaller sizes, and a great variety of colors.

Today's ideal Pomeranian should be a compact, short-coupled dog – exhibiting great intelligence in his expression and activity and buoyancy in his deportment. It should have two coats, a soft, fluffy undercoat and a long, straight overcoat; the hair at the neck should be especially profuse so that it forms a frill which extends over the shoulders. The hindquarters and legs should be covered with long hair or feathering from the top of the rump to the hocks. The characteristic tail is set high and carried flat over the back, with the tip curled. Self-colored dogs are preferred. Orange is most common, but all colors are acceptable, even particolors. The weight is about 4 to 5 pounds, and the height at the shoulder should not exceed 11 inches.

Right: Pomeranian.
Above right: Pointer.

Poodle *France*

Poodles (Caniches) come in three varieties: Standard (Caniches Grands), Miniature (Caniches Moyens), and Toy Poodles (Caniches Nains). The Standard Poodle came first, and was originally used as a gundog. It was, and is, a brilliant worker, although few of today's sophisticated Poodles have ever had – or are likely to get – the opportunity to prove their worth as sporting dogs. The outstanding features of the Poodle are its intelligence and its determination to please, and for centuries Poodles were a regular feature at French circus performances.

How long the breed has been established or where is not known. There are early reports of it in France, Germany, and Russia, and each of these countries has produced different colors: France white; Germany brown; Russia black. However, it is generally accepted that the Poodle is truly French, and that it is distantly related to the Foxhound and spaniel breeds. (In Standard Poodles of the more old-fashioned type, it is easy to see a relationship between the Poodle and Irish Water Spaniel.)

A typical Poodle is a very active, intelligent, and elegant-looking dog, well built, with a proud carriage; some would say he has an arrogant bearing. His head is carried high, and he has a fairly narrow skull and a long foreface with well-defined chin. The eyes are almond-shaped, dark brown, and slightly obliquely set. The body is strong, muscular, and not long; the tail is docked and carried at a slight angle away from the body. The coat is woolly but not

soft and thick all over. In adult show Poodles, the lion clip is normal. (In the United States this is known as the Continental clip and there are historic reasons for it. As a gundog the Poodle was used to retrieve duck from muddy lakes and ponds. So, to make swimming easier, the dog's hindquarters were shaved. Later, 'bobbles' were left on to protect the joints from rheumatism. The hair was also tied back from the eyes – first with string, later with colored ribbon so that it could be identified when swimming in muddy water.) The alternative clip, generally preferred, is the Dutch clip, a fairly close-cut body trim with baggy 'chaps' left on the legs.

Colors accepted in all countries are all solid colors. The white Poodle should have dark eyes, black nose, lips, and toenails; the brown Poodle should have dark amber eyes, dark liver nose, lips, and toenails; and the blue Poodle should have dark eyes, lips, and toenails. Regulations concerning sizes vary from country to country, but in Britain and the United States the measure for a Standard Poodle is 15 inches and over at the shoulder.

Miniature Poodles and Toy Poodles adhere to the same breed standard as that drawn up for the Standard Poodle; both Miniatures and Toys are, in fact, replicas in miniature of the Standard. The difference lies in the shoulder height, which for Miniatures should be under 15 inches and for Toys under 11 inches.

Above right: An apricot Toy Poodle.
Right: Silver Standard Poodle and Miniature Poodle (below).

Poodle-Pointer *Germany*

The Pudelpointer, a thoroughbred German dog, is descended from both the Poodle and the Pointer. In appearance it resembles the German Long-haired Pointer, and, as its name implies, it is employed as a gundog.

The Poodle-Pointer is a strong, compact-looking dog with a broad head, powerful foreface, and a pronounced stop. The ears are dropped and of medium size. The coat is coarse and particularly abundant around the eyes and on the chin, resulting in bushy eyebrows and whiskers.

The color is brown or golden brown, and the height at the shoulder varies between 21 and 26 inches.

Porcelaine *France*

Although the Porcelaine (Crockery) dog is officially recognized as a French breed, the Swiss regard the Porcelaine as their breed. It is descended from French hounds and English harriers and it is used as a tracker.

The Porcelaine gets its name from its smooth white and glossy coat, which is often decorated with small orange markings; these are especially profuse on the ears. The head is long and the eyes dark. The ears are also long and set fairly high. The tail is of medium length and carried in a slight curve.

The height at the shoulder varies between 22 and 23 inches for dogs.

Portuguese dogs *Portugal*

Mention has been made of the Perdiguero Portugués – the Portuguese Pointer – and the Podengo Portugués – the Portuguese Rabbit Dog. Other Portuguese breeds – little known outside the Iberian peninsula – are the Cão de Agua (Portuguese Water Dog), the Cão de Castro Laboreiro (Portuguese Guard Dog), the Cão da Serra de Aire (Portuguese Sheepdog), the Cão da Serra da Estrela (see *Estrela Mountain Dog*), and the Rafeiro do Alentejo (Portuguese Shepherd Dog).

The Cão de Agua is found principally in the Algarve, where, because of its swimming and diving ability, it is often used by fishermen to retrieve fish which have escaped from the hook, and as courier between boat and shore. It is related to both the Poodle and the Irish Water Spaniel.

The Cão de Castro Laboreiro is a Mastiff type and used mainly as a guard dog, as is the Rafeiro do Alentejo, which is the biggest of all the Portuguese breeds.

The Cão da Serra de Aire is a Portuguese sheepdog, an intelligent, lively animal, rectangular in shape with a large and

broad head and round, dark eyes. The breed bears a close resemblance to the better-known Bearded Collie.

Pug *Britain*

The Pug probably takes its name from an old English word used as a term of endearment for pets – pet monkeys in particular. The breed is believed to have originated in China and was a smooth-coated cousin of the Pekingese. However, while over the years the Peke became longer, lower, and hairier, the Pug became taller, heavier, and smoother. It was imported into England from the Netherlands in the middle of the nineteenth century and quickly became popular.

The Pug has changed little since it came to Europe. It is a decidedly square and compact little dog – an extrovert in temperament. Its color is pure black, fawn, or silver with a black mask, black ears, and a black trace along the back. The weight varies between 14 and 18 pounds and the height at the shoulder should not exceed 13 inches.

Top: Porcelaine.
Above: Portuguese Water Dog.
Right: Pug.

Puli *Hungary*

Few Hungarian breeds are found beyond the borders of their native land. The quaint little Puli, one of the four breeds of shepherd dogs in Hungary, is an exception. It is still a rarity in most countries, but when some Pulis were taken to the United States about 1930, its corded coat created a sensation and it has retained its popularity there.

Pulis are used in Hungary for hunting, particularly for duck shooting, and as sheepdogs. In Germany some have been successfully trained for police work. But in Britain and the United States they are kept mainly as pets and companions.

The Puli is a medium-sized dog, its main characteristic being its corded coat, which is long and wavy with a tendency to tangle. The head appears almost round on account of the plentiful hair, the eyes are slightly slanted with a bright expression, and the ears are dropped. The tail is carried curled over the back.

The color may be black, gray, or white. The height at the shoulder is 17 to 19 inches for dogs, 16 to 18 inches for bitches.

Pumi *Hungary*

Apart from the Puli, there are three other principal breeds of shepherd dogs in Hungary – the Komondor, Kuvasz, and the Pumi. Like the Puli, to which it is related, the Pumi was used mainly as a sheepdog and as a hunter; now it is used primarily as a guard dog.

The Pumi is a lively animal with a long, powerful foreface and semierect ears. The eyes are dark and slightly slanting. The tail is carried in line with the back, or slightly lower, and is docked to two-thirds of its natural length. The coat is profuse, wavy, but coarse.

Several colors are acceptable, but various shades of gray are most usual. The height at the shoulder is 15 to 17 inches.

Pyrenean Mountain Dog *France*

The Pyrenean Mountain Dog (Chien des Pyrénées) is a massive and magnificent animal, on a par with the Newfoundland and the St Bernard. For centuries it has been used as a guard and watch dog on the great estates in the border country between France and Spain. However, his gentleness, docility, faithfulness, and devotion to his master, as well as courage in the protection of anything placed in his care, makes the Pyrenean an ideal companion and pet. In consequence, before the French Revolution the Pyrenean enjoyed a brief interval as a sort of official court dog.

The Pyrenean is an elegant dog of immense size, keen intelligence, and kindly expression. It has a characteristic rolling, ambling gait and a profuse coat created to withstand severe weather. The color is white or predominantly white with badger, gray, or light tan markings. Dogs stand 27 to 32 inches at the shoulder, bitches 25 to 29 inches. The weight for dogs is between 100 and 125 pounds, 90 and 115 pounds for bitches.

Pyrenean Sheepdog *France*

The Pyrenean is one of the four principal

varieties of French sheepdogs. (The others are the Beauceron, Briard and Picardy). It is the smallest of these varieties and possibly the most vigorous. Some say it is a miniature Briard. It is found mainly in the area between the Pyrenees and Black Mountains. For a sheepdog the Pyrenean is quite tiny, being only 16 to 20 inches high. The color is usually fawn, but gray is quite common.

Right: Pyrenean Mountain Dog.
Below: Puli.

Rafeiro do Alentejo *Portugal*
This is a Portuguese herding dog, hailing
from the Alentejo province south of Lisbon.
It resembles the smooth-haired St Bernard
but has a lighter build. Its coat may be of
medium length or short. Colors are black,
gray, cream, or fawn with white markings.
The height at the shoulder is 26 to 29
inches for dogs, 25 to 28 inches for bitches.

Rastreador Brasileiro, see
Brazilian Tracker
The Brazilian Rastreador Hound is the
result of interbreeding between mainly the
American Foxhound and the Coonhound,
and it is said to be a very hardy animal.

Redbone Hound *USA*
The Redbone, named after his coloring, is
one of six varieties of Coonhound existing
in the United States. The breed is descended from American Foxhound stock,
with possibly a Bloodhound cross. In
America it is used extensively as a coon
hunter and also to 'tree' bear, cougar, and
other big game.
   Being lighter and leggier than the common Foxhound, the Redbone cannot be
said to resemble its forebears, nor is there
much evidence of its distant Bloodhound
relatives. The color is invariably red, with a
small amount of white on the chest and
feet. The weight is 45 to 60 pounds; the
height at the shoulder is 21 to 26 inches.

Rhodesian Ridgeback *South Africa*
The Rhodesian Ridgeback is now regarded
as the national breed of South Africa. It is
a strong, muscular, and active dog whose
tough and vicious ancestors were used to
hunt lions. The origins of the breed are
unknown but it probably stems from crossbreeding between native African dogs and
animals taken to Africa by the Europeans.
The peculiarity of the breed is the ridge
on the back, which is formed by the hair
growing in the opposite direction to the
rest of the coat. The ridge is normally
clearly defined, tapering, and symmetrical
– starting between the shoulders and con-
tinuing up to the hip bones. The Ridgeback's head is of moderate length and
rather broad. The eyes are round and
sparkling and the ears are carried close to
the head. The coat is short, thick, and
glossy. Color is light red wheaten, sometimes with a small white spot on the chest.
The height at the shoulder for dogs is 25 to
27 inches, bitches 24 to 26 inches. The
weight is about 80 pounds for dogs, 70
pounds for bitches.

Above and right: Rhodesian Ridgebacks.

Rottweiler *Germany*

The Rottweiler gets its name from the town of Rottweil in the Swabian Alps. Some 2000 years ago the Romans used the Rottweiler's ancestors to herd cattle over the St Gotthard Pass in order to supply the Roman legions invading Europe. Subsequently some of these cattledogs found their way up into Württemberg where – long after Caesar's legions had been recalled to Rome – the descendants of the Roman cattledogs were employed not only to herd cattle but as guard dogs. More recently they have been trained and employed as police dogs and war dogs.

In appearance the Rottweiler looks like a coarser and heavier version of the Dobermann. But, except for color and possibly temperament, the two breeds have little in common. If anything the Rottweiler is more docile and phlegmatic. The Rottweiler's stocky build does not prevent it from being agile. The head is fairly broad and rounded, the foreface powerful, and the ears small and triangular in shape. The neck and body display strength and power. The tail is docked short and carried in line with the back. The coat is close and short, slightly longer on legs and tail.

The color is black with clearly defined tan markings. The weight is 80 to 90 pounds. The height at the shoulder 22 to 27 inches.

Rough Collie *Britain*

The Rough Collie, sometimes called the Scotch Collie, is the popular sheepdog of the Scottish Highlands. Originally it was an insignificant farm dog, one among many, but as the best ones were picked as sheepdogs the type gradually stabilized. The British began to realize its merits when Queen Victoria bred Collies and encouraged an interest in improving them.

The Rough Collie is elegant and active, but also strongly built. The color is usually sable and white, tricolor or blue merle (a marbled blue with white). The height at the shoulder is 22 to 24 inches for dogs, 20 to 22 inches for bitches. The weight is 40 to 65 pounds.

Ruby, see Cavalier King Charles Spaniel and King Charles Spaniel

Russian Wolfhound, see Borzoi

Sabuesco Español *Spain*

This is a Spanish hound breed. Apart from tracking game or driving it on to the guns, it is used as a guard and police dog. There are two types – the Common and the Lesser. Both are broad and heavy in the head, with light or dark chestnut-colored eyes, long ears, and a tail carried in a slight downward curve. The color is white with large patches in orange and black. The height at the shoulder for the Common Sabuesco Español is 20 to 22 inches for dogs, 19 to 20 inches for bitches. The Lesser variety should not exceed 20 inches and 19 inches respectively.

Right: Rottweiler.
Below: Blue merle Rough Collie.

St Bernard *Switzerland*

The large and handsome breed known as St Bernard, or Great St Bernard, is so-called because for centuries it has been bred at the Hospice of St Bernard at the Great St Bernard Pass in Switzerland. They were trained to track travellers lost in the snow, and over the years they have become the centerpiece of numerous stories associated with the rescue of people buried in Alpine snow drifts. Most of the stories are pure fiction, although it is a fact that the monks of the St Bernard Hospice made good use of their dogs to find people lost in the snow and escort them to safety. Nowadays the St Bernard as a mountain rescue dog is virtually redundant, but it has found another purpose in life – as a pet. It is a big and heavy dog, but it has docile manners and is fairly easy to keep as such.

There are, in fact, two varieties of St Bernard – smooth and rough-haired. The difference, as the names suggest, is only in the coat. In rough specimens this should be dense and flat and rather fuller around the neck. With the smooth variety it should be close and hound-like, slightly feathered on the thighs and tail. Apart from this one could summarize the breed standard by saying that the St Bernard is a large, heavy dog with a massive head and kindly, dark, rimmed eyes deep-set. The color is usually white and orange. The height at the shoulder for dogs is at least 28 inches, preferably more, and bitches slightly less.

Saluki *Arabia*

The Saluki, 'Arabian' or 'Gazelle' Hound is the oldest of the Greyhound varieties, and is unique in the canine world since for thousands of years it has remained pure and been kept from interbreeding. Representations of the Saluki dating back to about 6000 BC illustrate that many of the finer points required of show dogs today were evident in the breed even then.

Since ancient times the Saluki has been the prized companion of the desert Bedouins, well adapted as it is for work as a hound in the dry, burning desert. Moslems regard dogs as 'unclean,' but make an exception for the highly valued Saluki, which may even be permitted to share its owner's quarters. In the West, the Saluki is kept almost exclusively as a pet. It moves very quickly and needs considerable exercise.

The body is lithe and graceful, the head finely chiselled and proudly carried. The coat is smooth and silky with long feathering on the ears and on the long, low-carried tail. Colors and sizes vary a great deal; dogs stand 23 to 28 inches at the shoulder, while bitches are proportionately smaller.

There is also a smooth-coated variety of the Saluki which completely lacks feathering on ears and tail, but is in all other respects the same.

Above: Saluki.
Right: St Bernard.

Samoyed *Arctic Siberia*

The Samoyed is a spitz breed which takes its name from a Siberian tribe called the Samoyedes. It was introduced to the West considerably earlier than other Arctic spitz breeds and was very popular in Britain even at the beginning of this century.

The typical show Samoyed is an affectionate and handsome creature, but full of action. It exudes serenity, power, and self-confidence. The head is powerful and wedge-shaped, the eyes almond-shaped and set well apart. The ears are erect and slightly rounded at the tips. The tail, not as tightly curled as in most other spitz breeds, is carried over the back when the dog is alert. The coat is very profuse, especially around the neck, on the tail, and on the feet.

The color is usually pure white, white and biscuit, or cream. The height at the shoulder is about 20 to 22 inches for dogs, 18 to 20 inches for bitches. The weight is 45 to 55 pounds for dogs, 36 to 45 pounds for bitches.

Sanshu *Japan*

The Sanshu is a medium-sized Japanese spitz breed which shares its ancestry with the Chow Chow. In Japan the breed is used both as a guard dog and as a pet.

The Sanshu is almost square in build with a broad, flat skull and dark, almond-shaped eyes. The tail is curled over the back. The coat is smooth, short, and coarse to the touch.

Accepted colors are a rusty red, black and tan, tan, fawn, pepper and salt, and particolor. The height at the shoulder is about 20 inches – about 1 inch less for bitches, 1 inch or so more for dogs.

Sar Planina *Yugoslavia*

The Sar Planina might be considered one of the rarer breeds insofar as it is rarely found outside its native country, and even there it is not often seen at dog shows. But in the mountainous regions of Yugoslavia it has been used as a cattledog for centuries. In conformation the Sar Planina resembles the German Hovawart. The head is slightly convex with a hardly perceptible stop, a long, powerful foreface, and dark, oval eyes. The ears are of medium size and dropped and the tail – which is sometimes docked – is set high and carried in an upward curve. The coat is thick and abundant and shorter on the head and legs, but particularly profuse on the tail.

The color is gray, possibly with some white on the legs or the chest. The height at the shoulder is about 22 to 23 inches.

Schipperke *Belgium*

The Schipperke's name is Belgian, and it has been translated as 'Little Boatman,' 'Little Skipper,' 'Little Captain,' and even 'Little Corporal.' The Schipperke's origin is, like that of so many breeds, shrouded in mystery, but some Schipperke historians believe that it is descended from two black, tailless dogs which were supposed to have saved William of Orange from an assassin. In the event the breed did not come into its own until about 100 years ago when British breeders took an interest in its development. Since then the Schipperke has gained considerable popularity, although it is still not particularly common.

The Schipperke's main characteristics are an intensively lively temperament, a fox-like head with a pointed foreface, and stiffly erect ears. The eyes are small and dark brown, the body short and deep. It has no tail. (Puppies are occasionally born with a tail but this is an indication of poor blood somewhere in the bloodline.) The coat, which is close and rough, forms a thick ruff around the neck and 'trousers' on the thighs.

The color is usually black, but other whole colors are acceptable. The weight is up to 18 pounds. The height at the shoulder should not exceed 12 inches.

Right: Samoyed.
Below: Schipperke.

Schnauzer *Germany*

There are three varieties of Schnauzer – the Giant Schnauzer (known in Germany nowadays as the Riesenschnauzer, but formerly as the Münchener Dog), the Standard Schnauzer (Schnauzer), and the Miniature Schnauzer (Zwergschnauzer). The name comes from *schnauze*, meaning snout or muzzle, and the word *schnauzbart* is used to describe a moustache or a man with a moustache. And all three varieties of Schnauzer have conspicuous moustaches.

The two smaller varieties are Germany's equivalent of the British terrier breeds. Although the Giant is virtually a bigger version of the Standard and Miniature, its forebears were sheepdogs and cattledogs in South Bavaria, subsequently mixed with other breeds. The Standard Schnauzer, on the other hand, is believed to have evolved from rough-coated dogs which were ratters – some say from crosses of the now extinct Schäferpudel and the Wire-haired German Pinscher. Both the Standard and the Miniature are outstanding ratters, but the Miniature is more than a dwarfed Standard. It was evolved from crosses of Standard Schnauzers with Affenpinschers.

Apart from size and weight requirements, the breed standard is the same for all three varieties of Schnauzer. All are clean-cut, powerful, square-built dogs with a temperament combining high spirits, reliability, endurance, and vigor. All have the characteristic moustache and beard, and all have tough, wiry, and dense coats. Colors are pure black or pepper and salt with a darker mark round the muzzle. In Germany the ears may be cropped. Standard Schnauzer dogs stand about 19 inches at the shoulder, bitches 18 inches; Giant Schnauzers normally range from 21 to 25 inches, but some dogs reach 27 inches; with Miniature Schnauzers the height should not exceed 14 inches for dogs (13 inches for bitches).

Scotch Collie, see **Rough Collie**

Scotch Greyhound, see **Deerhound**

Right, above and below: Standard and Giant Schnauzers.
Below: Miniature Schnauzer.

Scottish Terrier *Britain*

The sturdy, thick-set little 'Scottie' has long been regarded as symbolically Scottish. (In fact, the West Highland and the Cairn are equally representative of Scotland – if not more so.) Of all the terrier varieties existing in northern England and Scotland it is probably the most popular. Despite its small size and short legs, the Scottish Terrier is very active and surprisingly agile. The head is long, the nose large and black, and the deeply set eyes under the bushy eyebrows are extremely expressive. The coat is very coarse, thick, and wiry.

The color ranges from black, wheaten, to brindle. (The American standard also includes steel or iron gray, grizzled, or sandy.) The height at the shoulder is 10 to 11 inches, weight 19 to 23 pounds (Britain).

Sealyham Terrier *Britain*

In the middle of the nineteenth century, an eccentric sportsman by the name of John Owen Tucker Edwardes set out to breed terriers for hunting. From the local terriers near his estate at Sealyham in Wales the most vicious were selected and crossed with various other breeds to produce dogs that were small and game, capable of galloping with hounds and having the courage to stand up to fierce and cornered animals regardless of any disparity in size. Only the most vicious were allowed to survive; those who failed the stringent tests through which Captain Owen put them were shot out of hand. Not surprisingly, the original terriers of Sealyham were tough. Nowadays, although the present Sealyham is still hardy and obstinate, it has mellowed and has an astonishingly kindly temperament.

The Sealyham is an active, energetic, and strong dog. Despite its small size it is very heavily built and sturdy without appearing clumsy. The color is white, with or without lemon or brownish markings on the head and ears. The height at the shoulder should not exceed 12 inches. The weight for dogs is 20 pounds maximum, 18 pounds for bitches.

Segugio Italiano *Italy*

The Italian Segugio is related to the northern European breeds of foxhounds and harriers. Except for its long, thin, pendulous ears, it might be mistaken for a Greyhound, but is much more elegant.

Its head is long and narrow, the bridge of the nose is slightly convex, and the eyes are dark ocher in color. The tail is thin and gracefully carried in a saber-shaped curve. There are smooth-haired and wire-haired varieties.

The color is a red fawn in various shades or black and tan. The height at the shoulder is 21 to 23 inches for dogs, 19 to 22 inches for bitches.

Shetland Sheepdog *Britain*

The graceful little Shetland Sheepdog is in effect a miniature Rough Collie. For centuries it was used as a working dog on the Shetland Isles, and its small size can be attributed to the rugged and hostile environment there. (The term 'miniature' Collie is sometimes used in relation to this breed but the original dogs were not bantamized in order to satisfy the modern craving for 'toy' dogs, although no doubt the size has been kept small by selective breeding.)

Apart from its moderate size, the 'Sheltie' possesses an affectionate and friendly temperament and this makes it ideally suitable as a pet. It is an alert, gentle, and intelligent animal. The head is virtually a smaller copy of the Rough Collie. The coat is profuse. The color is usually sable with white markings, but there are several other varieties. The height at the shoulder is 14 inches for dogs, a bit less for bitches.

Right: Shetland Sheepdogs.
Below: Scottish Terrier.
Bottom: Sealyham Terrier.

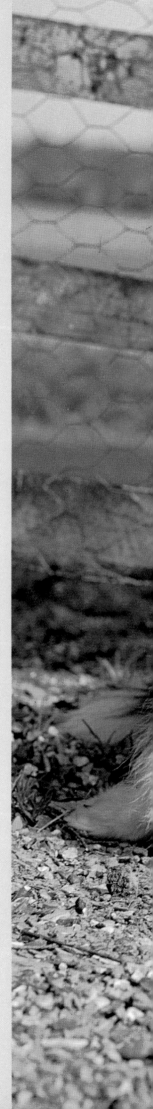

Shiba *Japan*

The Shiba is a Japanese spitz breed which is used primarily as a guard dog, although its temperament is generally friendly. It has a short, broad skull with a pointed face, dark brown eyes, small, triangular, pricked ears, and a body that is deep without being too short. The coat is rough, coarse, and straight. The tail may be curled, but a docked tail or a naturally bobbed tail is also acceptable. The color is red, salt and pepper, black, black and tan, or white.

The height at the shoulder for dogs is 15 to 16 inches, 14 to 15 inches for bitches.

Shih Tzu *Tibet*

Shih Tzu means 'lion dog' in Chinese, and the similarity between this breed and the Pekingese is so marked that it is obvious the Shih Tzu has been associated with China. In fact, the origins of the breed are Tibetan, and, like its Chinese cousin, it was kept as a temple dog. Unlike the Pekingese, however, it has developed a very open and outgoing temperament. Strictly speaking, it is neither a terrier nor a toy dog but, in spite of the grooming it requires, it is one of the most popular miniature breeds.

The Shih Tzu is a very active, lively, and alert little dog with a very long, thick, and straight coat. The hair is particularly abundant on the head and ears and grows upward on the nose, giving the head the typical 'chrysanthemum-like' effect. The muzzle is square and short but not wrinkled like a Pekingese.

All colors are acceptable, but a white blaze on the forehead and a white tip to the tail are highly prized. The height at the shoulder varies considerably, but is preferably just under 12 inches. The weight is up to 18 pounds – ideally 9 to 16 pounds.

Siberian Husky *USSR – Siberia*

There are two theories regarding the origin of the name 'Husky.' One is that it derives from Chukchi or Chuchi – the name of an Eskimo tribe living in the Kolyma River region of Siberia, the other is that the name is taken from the nomadic Tuski or Tchutski tribe, who also come from Siberia. In the past both tribes have used teams of these Arctic spitz-type dogs to pull sledges. But the Siberian Husky is comparatively more 'civilized' and friendly toward man than other Arctic spitz breeds, and in consequence has assumed the role of companion and pet – a role rarely enjoyed by other sledge dogs until modern

Above: Siberian Husky.
Right: Shih Tzu.

times. More recently he has been used in Alaska as a racer in sweepstake contests to track a snow-bound course, sometimes 400 miles long.

The Siberian Husky has a powerful and well-muscled body. His head is typical of the spitz, with erect ears and an alert expression, and the heavily haired tail is carried over the back in a sickle curve; when the dog is at rest, the tail is dropped. The coat is thick, fairly long, hangs loosely from the body, and is surprisingly soft.

All colors are acceptable. Most common is silver gray or tan with white markings. The height at the shoulder for dogs is 21 to 24 inches, 20 to 22 inches for bitches.

Silky Terrier *Australia*

The Australian Silky Terrier, sometimes known as the 'Sydney Terrier,' is not, as its name implies, a terrier at all but a member of the toy group. Nor is its ancestry Australian, but British, although the breed was developed in Sydney, New South Wales. It emerged as the result of crosses between the Australian Terrier and various other terrier and toy dog varieties, including the Yorkshire Terrier which is responsible for two of the features separating the Australian Terrier from the Silky Terrier. These are the Silky Terrier's fairly long, thick, and silky coat, which is quite straight, and its body, which is more compact and shorter than the Australian Terrier's. (Mature dogs have a coat of 5 to 6 inches long from behind the ears to the base of the tail.) The Silky Terrier is slightly smaller than the Australian Terrier and stands about 9 inches at the shoulder. The color is blue and tan, but the blue may be silver blue, pigeon, or slate blue and the tan deep and rich.

Skye Terrier *Britain*

The Skye Terrier is a one-man dog, not vicious but distrustful of strangers. Originally it had much in common with the Scottish Terrier – the first Skye Terriers did, in fact, compete in the same classes as its now more common relatives. The Skye Terrier is a heavily built dog with a long, low body, and at dog shows its long, straight coat flowing from a parting along the spine invariably attracts attention. The head is long with powerful jaws; the nose is black. The ears can be either pricked or dropped; the long tail is carried low and gracefully feathered. The color is blue gray, fawn, or cream with black points. The height at the shoulder is about 10 inches; the total length (nose to tip of tail) is about 41 inches; and weight averages about 25 pounds.

Slovakian Kopov *Czechoslovakia*

The Slovakian Kopov (Slovensky Kopov) is a hound – the only hunting breed of its kind in Czechoslovakia. It is descended from a variety of different hounds which existed several hundred years ago in Central Europe and has evolved as a separate breed with a reputation for toughness and agility.

The Slovakian Kopov is of medium size and thick-set build. The head is long, the jaws powerful, the ears fairly large and carried close to the head. The length of the Kopov's back is greater than its height at the shoulder. The tail is thick, of medium length, and well covered with coarse hair, but not forming a fringe. The coat is 1 to 2 inches long.

The color is black with brown markings above the eyes, on the cheeks, feet, lower parts of the legs, and around the vent. The height at the shoulder for dogs is 18 to 20 inches, 16 to 18 inches for bitches.

Slovakian Kuvasz *Czechoslovakia*

The Slovakian Kuvasz (Slovensky Cuvac) is believed to be related to the more common Hungarian Kuvasz, but it also resembles the Polish Owczarek Podhalanski. (Both the Polish and Slovakian breeds are sometimes known as Tatra dogs – after the mountain range which runs through both countries and where the two breeds have existed for a long time.)

Despite its smaller stature, the Slovakian breed is as imposing as its relatives such as the Pyrenean Mountain Dog and the Maremma sheepdog. It is heavily boned, has a lively temperament, and is alert, courageous, and intelligent.

Originally only white animals were bred so that the dog could be easily distinguished from beasts of prey in the darkness. Pure white is still the most desirable color, though an off-white shade is acceptable.

The height at the shoulder is around 24 inches, but should not exceed 28 inches for dogs or 26 inches for bitches.

Slughi *Morocco*

The Slughi is one of the Eastern Greyhound breeds, probably the most rare of the sighthound breeds in the West. It is sometimes confused with a Saluki, which is medium-coated and feathered while the Slughi is always smooth-coated and has a slightly heavier build. The color is usually sandy, sometimes brindle. The height at the shoulder is 22 to 30 inches.

Far right: Australian Silky Terrier.
Right: Slughi.
Below: Skye Terrier.

Smalandsstövare *Sweden*

The Smalandsstövare is a hound used for tracking game in Scandinavia. The breed gets its name from the Smaland region, where these dogs were probably first used.

The Smalandsstövare is an active and agile dog, strongly built but not heavy. The foreface is neither broad nor sharp and the eyes are dark. The ears, which are carried close to the head, are soft and rounded at the tips. The tail is either short or long and is either straight or slightly curved. The color is black with tan markings above the eyes, on the feet, and under the tail. Dogs stand about 20 inches at the shoulder, bitches 18 inches.

Smooth Collie *Britain*

To most people 'Collie' refers to a Rough Collie. The layman is generally surprised to learn that there are several types, and that one variety is smooth-coated. The Smooth Collie is comparatively rare both in Britain and outside its home country. With the exception of the coat, it conforms to the standard of the Rough Collie.

Soft-coated Wheaten Terrier *Eire*

The Soft-coated Wheaten Terrier is a native of Ireland, where it has been used for a variety of purposes ranging from driving cattle, guard dog, to ratter. The breed may be descended from the long-extinct English Black and Tan Terrier, and it is a relative of both the Irish and Kerry Blue Terriers. The breed has been known for several centuries but it is now relatively rare even in Ireland.

The Soft-coated Wheaten Terrier is a strong, active dog with a lovable disposition. It has a compact and short body without exaggerated features. The head is moderately long with small, well-fringed, thin ears folded forward. The eyes are dark with an intelligent expression and the whole body is covered with a profuse, soft coat – wavy or with large, loose curls.

The color is usually a light wheaten. The height at the shoulder is about 18 inches and the weight is 35 to 40 pounds.

Spanish Mastiff *Spain*

The Spanish Mastiff, the Mastin Español, is also known as the Mastin de Estremadura or Mastin de la Mancha. Like its British counterpart, it is a large, heavily built dog giving the impression of grandeur and power. The head is broad with a rounded skull, well-defined stop, and small ears dropping forward to the cheek. The tail is thick and fairly short, carried low in repose and slightly curved in action. The hind legs are broad, wide, and muscular.

Above: Spinone.
Right: Soft-coated Wheaten Terrier.
Far right: Smooth Collie.

There are several color varieties: most common are gray, fawn, brindle, or white with black, fawn, or gray markings. The weight is usually about 110 to 132 pounds. The height at the shoulder is 26 to 28 inches for dogs, considerably less for bitches.

Spinone *Italy*

The Spinone, the Italian Pointer, has a good deal in common with the British Pointer, but it is said to be slower in the field than the British dog. It is descended from the old European hunting dogs, the Griffons, which have contributed to the bloodlines of many modern gundog breeds.

In conformation, the Italian Pointer is slightly heavier and coarser than the English Pointer. The head is large with a fairly broad and domed skull, the stop is not very accentuated, but the muzzle is well developed and square. The nose is brown, light brown, or liver with well-expanded nostrils. The ears are large and carried close to the head. The eyes, under bushy eyebrows, are light brown or yellow and they have an alert expression. The back is slightly arched over the loin and the chest is deep but not broad. The feet are round and the toes well knuckled up. The tail is carried in line with, or slightly above, the back. The coat is short, hard, and wiry.

The Spinone is either pure white, or white with small lemon or light brown markings. The height at the shoulder varies considerably, from 24 to 28 inches for dogs to 23 to 26 inches for bitches.

Spitz breeds

The spitz group is one of the main families of dogs, believed to be descended from the 'Peat Dog' or 'Swiss Lake Dwellers Dog' of 6000 years ago. The best-known breeds are listed separately in this catalog of breeds: they include the Siberian Husky, Alaskan Malamute, Samoyed, Eskimo, Keeshond, Norwegian Elkhound, Pomeranian, Chow Chow, and Schipperke.

Springer Spaniel, see English Springer Spaniel and Welsh Springer Spaniel

Stabyhoun *Netherlands*

The Stabyhoun is a pointing gundog with a temperament which makes it as suitable as a domestic pet as for employment in the field. The Stabyhoun is of rectangular build and is neither very graceful nor heavy. The eyes are dark in black roan types but are often lighter in other color varieties. The tail is long and well feathered, the lower third curving upward. The coat is long and flat without curl.

The color is usually white with black, blue, liver, or orange markings. The height at the shoulder is approximately 20 inches for dogs.

Staffordshire Bull Terrier *Britain*

The Staffordshire Bull Terrier is not one of the most popular terrier breeds, although it has a large following in its home country, Britain, and in the United States. Such dogs are noted for their indomitable courage, their high intelligence, and tenacity. These qualities coupled with affection for their friends – children in particular – and trustworthy stability make them all-purpose dogs. Originally they were used as guard and fighting dogs; nowadays they are mainly pets and companions.

The Staffordshire Bull Terrier is a smooth-coated dog which greatly resembles the Bull Terrier, although it does not have the latter's sweeping lines and head shape. It is a medium-sized, fairly long-legged terrier, heavily built and thick-set. The head is broad with a marked stop and half-pricked or 'rose' ears. The coat is short and glossy, and close to the skin.

The color ranges from particolor to brindle or whole-color in a variety of shades. The height at the shoulder is 14 to 16 inches. The weight for dogs is 28 to 38 pounds, bitches 24 to 34 pounds.

Staffordshire Terrier *USA*

The Staffordshire Terrier, which should not be confused with the Staffordshire Bull Terrier, is a wholly American breed. It is related to the Staffordshire Bull Terrier in that both breeds had a common origin in Bulldog and terrier crosses. The American dog is taller, however, and generally looks more like a true terrier than the Staffordshire Bull. Originally it was bred for fighting and around 1900 was known as the 'American Pit Bull Terrier' or 'Yankee Terrier'; subsequently the name was changed to American (Pit) Bull Terrier, and only since 1936, when the breed was recognized by the American Kennel Club, has it been known as the Staffordshire Terrier.

The Staffordshire Terrier has a deep head of medium length, with a moderate muzzle and very pronounced cheek muscles. The eyes should be dark and round. For show purposes the ears are erect and cropped; if uncropped they should be 'rose' or pricked, but never dropped. The front legs are set wide apart to permit a powerful chest; the hindquarters are powerfully muscled and the feet are compact. The tail is short and set on low. The breed comes in all colors; the height is 17 to 19 inches.

Stag hounds

Stag hunting is one of the world's oldest hunting sports in which dogs are used. It is now also one of the rarest sports, being practiced today in only a few places in Britain. (Hunting deer with dogs is prohibited in the United States.) Hounds bred purely for stag hunting are now extinct and the only modern dog with a stag-hunting history is the Scottish Deerhound.

Steinbracke *Germany*

The Steinbracke is one of the less common members of the German 'bracke' group, and is similar in conformation to the Westfälische Dachsbracke. The breed is described as being of 'medium' size and invariably tricolor.

Steirischer Rauhaariger Hochgebirgsbracke *Austria*

This Austrian 'bracke' (hound) is similar to the more common German bracke breeds, but it is wire-haired and slightly bigger. Its eyes are dark brown or yellow, the ears are dropped and, as distinct from the rest of the body, are covered with short, soft hair. The tail is curved saber-fashion with a tuft of hair at the tip. The color is red or pale fawn, sometimes with a small white spot on the chest. The height at the shoulder is 16 to 20 inches.

Above: Staffordshire Bull Terrier.
Above right: Sussex Spaniel.

Sussex Spaniel *Britain*

The massive and strongly built Sussex
Spaniel is, unfortunately, becoming something of a rarity. As an established breed it
has existed since the eighteenth century,
having been evolved by crossing various
existing spaniels. (The purpose was to
develop a dog for rough-shooting sportsmen in districts where the undergrowth
was dense and impenetrable – a strong,
stolid dog with a penetrating 'voice.') By
the end of World War II, however, the
number of dogs available for breeding in
both Britain and the United States had
dropped to single figures, so to avoid too
much inbreeding it was sometimes neces-

sary to resort to outcrosses with other
spaniels. The net result is that the number
of true Sussex Spaniels has declined and it
would seem that the breed is in danger of
becoming extinct.

The Sussex Spaniel is an active, energetic,
and strong dog who moves unlike any other
spaniel with a characteristic roll. It is
similar in conformation to the Clumber
Spaniel but less heavy. Its eyes have a soft,
slightly wistful expression and its ears are
thicker than in most other spaniels. It has a
long back and its legs are strong and
muscular. The tail is docked, but not too
short, well feathered, and carried low. The
coat is profuse and sleek with feathering on

the legs, ears, and thighs.

The color is liver, shading to gold at the tips – a characteristic feature of the breed. The weight for dogs is about 45 pounds. The height at the shoulder is 15 to 16 inches.

Swedish Schillerstövare *Sweden*

The Swedish Schillerstövare is one of the hounds used in Scandinavia for tracking game. It resembles the Hamiltonstövare, but its ancestors were mostly dogs imported from Germany, Austria, and Switzerland. The main difference between the two breeds is that the Schillerstövare is slightly lighter than the Hamiltonstövare. Its head is fairly long with a marked stop and dark, luminous eyes; its ears are carried close to the head. The neck is long, the body powerful with a deep chest. The tail is straight or saber-shaped, the coat close and short.

The color is always tan with a black saddle. Dogs stand 20 to 24 inches at the shoulder, bitches 18 to 23 inches.

Swiss Laufhund *Switzerland*

The Swiss Laufhund (Schweizer Laufhund) is a foxhound breed which has become extremely popular, not only in its native land but elsewhere is Europe as well (especially in Norway).

It is an active, powerfully built, and friendly dog. It closely resembles the English Foxhound, but its head has a marked stop with a pronounced furrow in the middle. The eyes are dark and slanting; the ears, which are large, thin, and supple, are set lower than in most other harrier/foxhound breeds. The tail is carried high; the coat is smooth and short.

The color is predominantly white with lemon or orange patches. The height at the shoulder should be at least 16 inches.

Swiss Mountain Dog *Switzerland*

In its own country the Swiss Mountain Dog is known as the 'Large' Swiss Mountain Dog (Grosser Schweizer Sennenhund). Before railroads were built, it was used to drive cattle to market but, now that such cattledogs are no longer needed, the breed numbers have declined and the Large Swiss Mountain Dog is not very common outside Switzerland.

It is the biggest of the Swiss herding breeds – slightly taller, heavier, and more stolid than the Bernese Mountain Dog. Its ears are larger than those of the Bernese and carried dropped; its neck is long, thick, and muscular. Its body is broad, deep, and muscular and its tail is carried low.

The color is that of the other herding breeds – predominantly black with tan

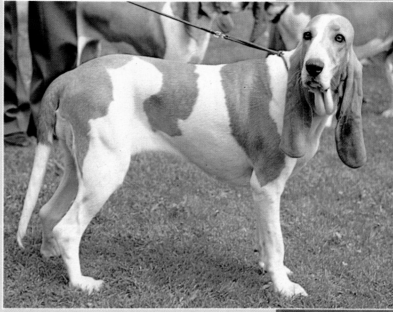

markings on the head, chest, and legs, a white blaze on the foreface, white throat and feet. The shoulder height is 25 to 28 inches for dogs, 23 to 26 inches for bitches.

Tervueren, see Belgian Tervueren

Tibetan Apso, see Lhasa Apso

Tibetan Spaniel *Tibet*

The little Tibetan Spaniel is a toy dog breed descended from the temple dogs of ancient Tibet and it is fairly rare. 'Spaniel,' of course, has a modern European flavor – originally all 'spaniels' were gundogs, but the name was given later to a few toy breeds which bore some resemblance to the spaniel proper, for example, King Charles Spaniels. However, the Tibetan Spaniel is not related in any way to spaniels; it can perhaps be described best as something between a Pekingese and a Shih Tzu.

It is an elegant little creature with a slightly domed head that is small in proportion to its body. Its ears are dropped like those of the Pekingese, but the eyes are not as large and prominent and the legs are longer and straighter. The tail is carried in a plume over the back and the coat is less profuse than that of the Pekingese.

Many colors are acceptable: white, cream, fawn, golden, brown, or black – whole-colors or particolors. The height at the shoulder for dogs should not exceed 11 inches or about 9 inches for bitches.

Tibetan Terrier *Tibet*

The Tibetan Terrier comes from Tibet, but it is certainly not a true terrier as it was

Above: Swiss Laufhund.
Right: Tibetan Spaniels.

not bred to go to ground. For this reason it is classed in Britain as one of the non-sporting dogs, like the Tibetan Spaniel and Shih Tzu. However, like all terriers, the Tibetan Terrier has an alert, game, and intelligent temperament; it is neither fierce nor pugnacious but it is usually chary of strangers.

In general appearance it is not unlike an Old English Sheepdog in miniature. Its head has a marked stop, a black nose, large dark eyes, and vee-shaped pendant ears. Its coat, which is profuse and either straight or wavy, is particularly abundant on the head. Its tail is of medium length, very well feathered, and carried in a gay curl over the back.

The color is usually white, gray, cream, or black, but may vary considerably. The height at the shoulder is 14 to 16 inches.

Trail Hound *Britain*

The Trail Hound, which is not recognized internationally as a breed, is a variety of crossbred foxhound. For generations it has been used in the north of England in trailing competitions over several miles where dogs follow a ground scent, and where speed, agility, and a good nose are all-important. A typical Trail Hound is all sinew and muscle; its short coat is shaved before competitions. The most common colors are black and white, fawn, or gray-and-white particolor. Height at the shoulder varies, but averages 22 to 26 inches.

Tyrolean Bracke *Austria*

The Tyroler Bracke is descended from a variety of local Austrian breeds and is used as a hunting dog. There are two types: the larger and smaller. The head is long and lightly boned with large, high-set, and pendulous ears and large eyes. The occiput is pronounced, especially in dogs. The tail is long and slightly curved. The coat is short. The basic color is black, red, or fawn, or tricolor. The height at the shoulder is 16 to 19 inches for the larger variety, 12 to 15 inches for the smaller.

Vastgotaspitz *Sweden*

The Vastgotaspitz is a short-legged, active, and alert little spitz which has been used for centuries in the south of Sweden as a cattledog. It is lighter than the Welsh Corgi which it resembles; its back is not as long and its legs not quite as short. The tail is short, often bobbed. The coat is hard, fairly short, and close.

The color varies from gray to fawn, with darker shadings on the back and lighter shadings on the underside of the body. Shoulder height is 13 to 16 inches.

Vizsla *Hungary*

The Vizsla, or Magyar Vizsla, is Hungary's most famous hunting dog. It is of general pointer type and comes in two varieties – Short-haired and Wire-haired (Drotszoru-vizsla). Of the two, the Short-haired variety is the more common and better known in countries other than Hungary; its main characteristic is probably the color of its coat – a 'rusty gold.' Also characteristic is the pale, liver-colored nose; the eyes are medium size and brown. In general conformation the Vizsla is more robust and less refined than the pointer, its head is coarser with larger ears and the tail is docked. In temperament it is lively, affectionate, and easy to train. Apart from rusty gold, the color may also be a sandy yellow in varying shades. The height at the shoulder is 22 to 24 inches for dogs, 21 to 23 inches for bitches.

The Wire-haired Vizsla was evolved by crossing Short-haired Vizslas with German Wire-haired Pointers. This breed is slightly bigger than the Short-haired variety, otherwise the only distinguishing feature is the texture of the coat which is rough and forms whiskers on the chin.

Volpino Italiano *Italy*

This is a diminutive little spitz which resembles the Pomeranian, although its ears are bigger and more pointed and the foreface is longer. Its coat is long and profuse; the color is always white or red without markings.

The height at the shoulder is 11 to 12 inches for dogs, 10 to 11 inches for bitches.

Right: Tibetan Terrier mother with babies.
Below right: Vastgotaspitz.
Below: Hungarian Vizsla.

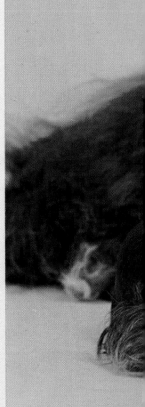

Wachtelhund *Germany*

The Wachtelhund, a German equivalent of the British spaniel, is used primarily as a water retriever and to track game.

In appearance it resembles the English Springer Spaniel, although the head is not so 'spaniel-like.' Apart from the muzzle not being so deep and square, the ears are not as big. Furthermore, the Wachtelhund's coat is wavy and more profuse – especially on the ears, neck, chest, underside of the body, at the back of the forelegs, and on the thighs. The color is usually liver. The height at the shoulder is 18 to 20 inches for dogs, 16 to 18 inches for bitches.

Weimaraner *Germany*

The Weimaraner is the most senior of the German sporting dogs. It is said to have been bred at Weimar toward the end of the eighteenth century by Grand Duke Carl August, who wanted some better all-purpose hunting dogs, and the Weimaraner Vorstehhund, or Weimar Pointer as it was first known, proved to be a super field dog.

It is a medium-sized, gray dog with a head rather like that of a pointer and light-colored eyes – in shades of amber, gray, or blue-gray. The Weimaraner's head is moderately long and aristocratic, but the lobular ears are larger and longer than those of the pointer and they are set high. The body is well developed and muscular, presenting a general appearance of power, stamina, alertness, and balance. There are Short-haired, Wire-haired, and Long-haired Weimaraners, but the Short-haired variety is the most common. The tail of the two former varieties is docked two-thirds from the root, while only the tip of the tail

Above: Cardigan Corgi.
Right: Weimaraner.

in the Long-haired type is removed.

The color varies from mouse gray to silver gray with lighter shades on the head and ears. The nose is gray, the lips and gums pinkish. The height at the shoulder is 23 to 25 inches for dogs, 22 to 24 inches for bitches.

Welsh Corgi, Cardigan *Britain*

Corgi is the old Celtic word for dog (after the Norman Conquest of Britain in 1066 the native Britons were prohibited from owning Norman dogs. Corgi was corrupted to curgi and finally to cur – a word used today to describe mongrels, the only type of animals available to Britons in the eleventh century.) It is not generally appreciated that there are two varieties: one, the Cardigan Corgi, is very rare outside Britain and not especially common even in its home country; the other variety, the Pembroke, is the one that most people are referring to when they speak of the Welsh Corgi.

The Cardigan Corgi is slightly bigger and heavier than the Pembroke and it is usually considered to have a calmer and quieter temperament. The head is moderately broad but foxy and the ears are larger and more rounded than those of the Pembroke. The tail is fairly long, resembling a fox brush, and set in line with the body – not curled over the back.

All colors except pure white are acceptable, but red or brindle with white markings, or blue merle, are most popular. The height at the shoulder is approximately 12 inches for a dog.

Welsh Corgi, Pembroke *Britain*

Today, if only because Corgis are the special favorites of Queen Elizabeth, the Pembrokeshire Corgi is probably the one spitz breed with the greatest claim to international fame.

The origin of the breed is in some doubt. It is said to have been taken to England by Flemish weavers about the turn of the twelfth century, and some of these weavers moved to South Wales, taking their dogs with them. They were bred by farmers for herding, and are the smallest of the working dogs. The Pembroke Corgi works by darting at the hind legs of cattle, nipping at their heels and barking to move the herd. Consequently these dogs are inclined to nip at the ankle. There is no question that the breed is descended from the old family of spitz dogs and it bears a striking resemblance to the Swedish Vastgotaspitz.

The Pembroke Welsh Corgi is the only British spitz. It is a sturdy, low-set, alert, and active dog with an intelligent and bold expression – slightly fox-like in appearance. Its head is carried proudly and its ears are medium-sized and slightly pointed. The body is rather long with a level back and short, heavily boned, straight legs. The tail is usually short by nature. The coat is of medium length and dense, not wiry. The color ranges from sable red to tricolor with white markings on legs, neck, and muzzle. The height at the shoulder is 10 to 12 inches, weight about 20 to 24 pounds.

Welsh Springer Spaniel *Britain*

The 'Welsh Spaniel' or 'Springer' is sometimes known in Wales as a 'Starter.' The breed, which is of very ancient and pure origin, was bred and preserved purely for working purposes. For 200 years or so it has remained practically free of foreign blood; nevertheless it does resemble the English Springer Spaniel.

The Welsh Springer is a spirited, compact, and very active dog, obviously built for endurance and hard work. The head, which is neither short nor chubby, differs from that of the English Springer in that it has shorter ears. The eyes are hazel or dark brown, the nose flesh-colored or black. The body is strong and muscular, the feet small and cat-like, and the tail is low-set and carried low. The coat is smooth, thick, and silky but not too profuse and with moderate feathering on the ears and back of the legs.

The color is always white with dark rich-red markings. The weight is about 35 to 45 pounds and height at shoulder about 16 inches.

Right: Pembroke Corgis.
Above right: Welsh Springer Spaniel.

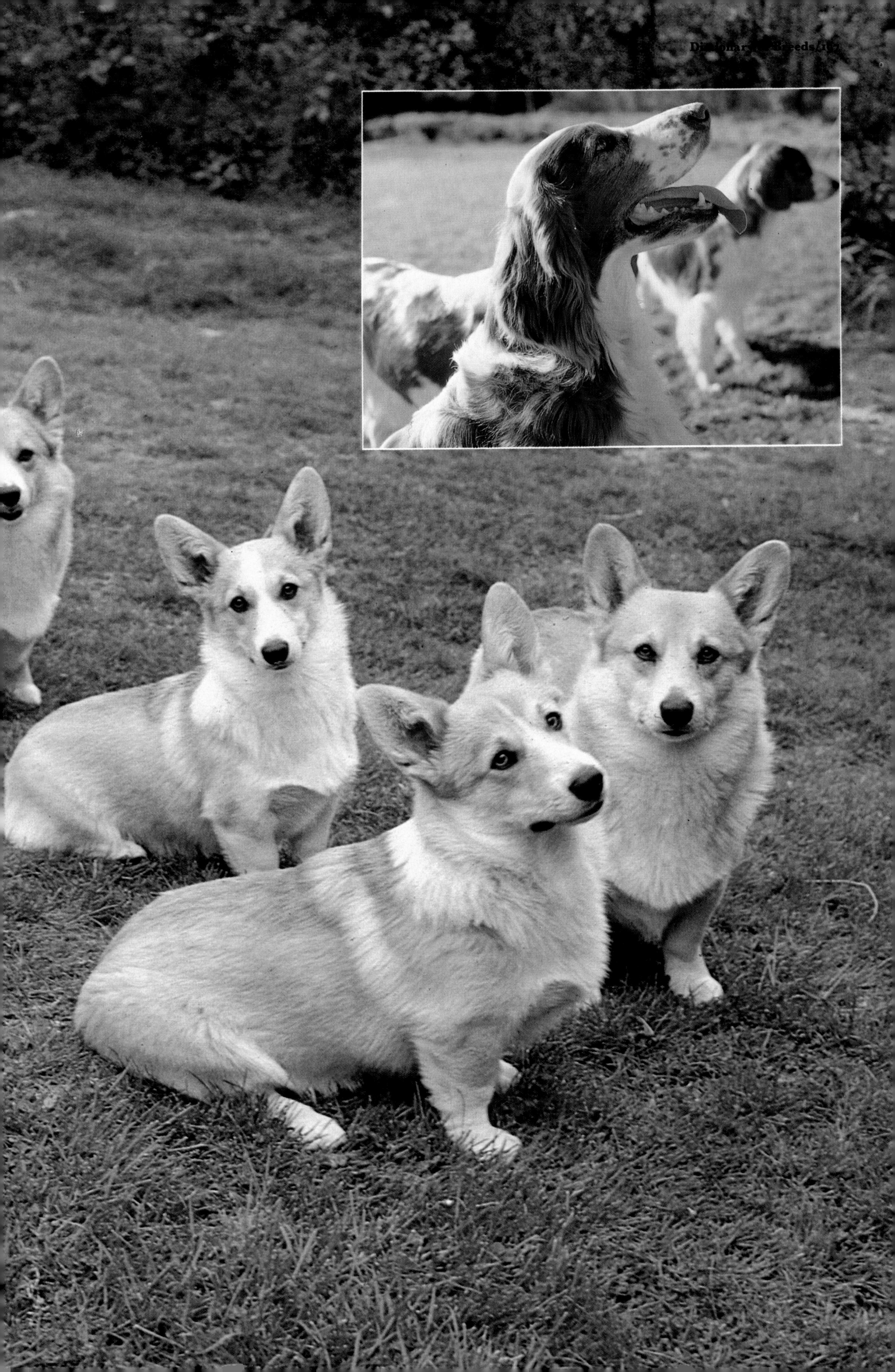

Welsh Terrier *Britain*

The Welsh Terrier is a dog with a dual nationality. The Welsh claim that it is a breed of great antiquity and as Welsh as the leek. On the other hand, the English reckon that it is descended from the Old English Wire-haired Black-and-Tan Terrier. In effect it could be said to be a sort of miniature Airedale, looking very much like a Fox Terrier and with Fox Terrier characteristics. It is a game and fearless little dog, affectionate, obedient, and easily controlled – qualities that make him an eminently suitable dog for town life. Furthermore, Welsh Terriers are normally of a hardy and robust constitution and need no pampering. They are easy to train and anxious to please.

The head of a Welsh Terrier is flatter and rather wider between the ears than the Wire-haired Fox Terrier, giving it more of a masculine appearance. The coat is coarse and wiry and the color is black and tan or black grizzle and tan. The height at the shoulder should not exceed $15\frac{1}{2}$ inches, and 20 to 21 pounds is considered to be the average weight.

Westfälische Dachsbracke, see Dachsbracke

West Highland White Terrier *Britain*

Scotland has five main breeds of terriers – Cairns, Dandie Dinmonts, Skyes, Scottish Terriers, and West Highland Whites. All of them are true Scots, and the Cairn is probably the oldest and still the most popular. But in recent years the West Highland White – which some say is merely a variety of Cairn into which Sealyham blood was introduced in the dim and distant past – has been steadily climbing the popularity ladder. It is a hardy breed but it has a friendly disposition and makes an ideal companion. It is a natural working dog and is fearless and persistent in chasing its prey.

The general appearance of the West Highland is that of a small, game, hardy-looking terrier. It has a short, compact body similar to that of the Scottish Terrier. However, the West Highland is not as low-set as the Scottie, nor is the head as long and, because of its abundant coat, the West Highland's skull appears to be completely round. The eyes are set wide apart and are sunk slightly into the head; the nose is black. The ears are small, pointed, and carried stiffly erect. The coat is profuse, about 2 inches long, straight, and hard except on the ears where it is smooth and velvety. The color is pure white and height at the shoulder is about 11 inches.

Wetterhoun *Netherlands*

The Wetterhoun is probably the only Dutch gundog which is found outside its homeland. Although it is known as the 'Dutch Spaniel,' it has little in common with the British spaniel breeds either in looks or temperament. In conformation the Wetterhoun is similar to the massive Newfoundland dog.

Depending on the color of its coat the Wetterhoun has dark or light chestnut-brown eyes. The ears are dropped, with the unusual characteristic of fairly long, wavy hair at the base which gradually becomes shorter and smoother toward the tip. The tail is spiral-shaped. The color is black, brown and white, or blue and white. Height at the shoulder for dogs is about 22 inches.

Right: West Highland White Terrier.
Below: Welsh Terrier.

Whippet *Britain*

The Whippet is believed to have evolved in Britain over the past three centuries. It probably descended from small greyhounds and various types of terriers, and it was even used early in its history for racing and rabbiting. In some Whippets the lively terrier blood is still apparent, while others have the quiet disposition typical of the Greyhound.

In conformation the Whippet is a smaller version of the Greyhound but with a slightly sturdier frame. The head is long and lean, the jaws powerful, and the eyes dark. The ears are fine in texture, with the tips folded when the dog is alert. The back is slightly arched over the loin with well-defined flanks. All in all it is a dog which gives a general impression of balanced muscular power combined with great elegance.

Fawn, brindle, and white in various combinations are the most common colors, but any color or mixture of colors is acceptable. The height at the shoulder is just over 18 inches for dogs and about 17 inches for bitches.

Wire-haired Pointing Griffon *France*

The Wire-haired Pointing Griffon, as it is called in the United States, is known under the name of Griffon d'Arrêt à Poil Dur in what is now regarded as its native country, France. It is a somewhat slow-working pointing dog and retriever with an excellent nose.

Credit for developing the breed is given to Eduard Korthals, who lived near Haarlem in Holland and later in Germany. Korthals combined different continental gundog breeds – mainly varieties of the French Water Spaniel – and evolved what was then known as the Korthals Griffon. The breed attracted considerable interest in France, partly because Korthals served as an agent for the Duke of Penthievre, and the Korthals Griffon was crossed with other French dogs before the breed was standardized. Although the resultant dogs were at one time very popular in Europe, they are rarely seen in France nowadays and hardly ever abroad except in the USA, where they were introduced at the turn of the century.

The American version of the Wire-haired Griffon is a heavily built, longish-legged dog. The head is long and narrow, the eyes large and amber or light brown. The ears are set high, carried dropped, of medium size, and sparsely coated. The nose is always brown. The body and legs are strong and muscular, and the tail docked to about one-third of its length and carried in line with the back or slightly above it. The coat is rough and shaggy without curl which gives the dog an ungroomed look. (There is also a long-haired variety, the Griffon à Poil Laineux.)

The color is steel gray or light gray with chestnut-colored patches. The height at the shoulder for dogs is about 22 inches, and 20 inches for bitches.

Xoloitzcuintli, see Hairless dogs

Yorkshire Terrier *Britain*

The Yorkshire Terrier is an attractive, long-coated toy breed which has retained the lively terrier temperament of its older relatives. As a recognized breed, the Yorkshire Terrier is of fairly recent origin, having evolved during the nineteenth century through attempts to create a new toy dog. Exactly how the British breeders concentrating on this achieved their objective is not known, but English Black-and-Tan Terriers and Maltese were probably used in fairly large numbers.

At one time the size of the dog and the length of its coat were considered of prime importance but now, fortunately, emphasis is also placed on soundness and a bright temperament. The coat should be long enough to reach the ground, which may present difficulties overcome only by keeping the coat protected by plastic bags or tied up in 'curlers.'

The steel blue color of the body coat should be pure and not intermingled with the tan markings on the head, chest, and legs. The weight should not exceed 7 pounds, while the height at the shoulder is about 8 inches.

Right: Whippets.
Below: Yorkshire Terrier.

RARE BREEDS

Previous page, left:
Anatolian Karabash Dog.
Previous page, right: Basset
Griffon Vendéen.

Some breeds of dog are numerically rare, while others may well be very common in their own country but virtually unknown elsewhere. The Czechoslovakian Cesky Terrier, for example, is an extremely rare terrier breed, while Anatolian Karabash Dogs, of which vast numbers are employed as sheepdogs, are rarely seen outside Turkey. Thus one's interpretation of the term 'rare' can depend on from where one is reviewing the canine world. In the following pages the two categories are considered together and it is hoped that the brief description of the breeds concerned may prove to be of interest to readers.

Aidi *Morocco*

The Aidi, a breed which is almost completely unknown outside Morocco, makes an excellent guard dog. Its origin is unknown, but it is probable that its ancestors were European mountain dogs taken across the Straits of Gibraltar and allowed to spread in the Atlas Mountain region.

The Aidi is a powerful, bold, and active dog with a piercing expression, which carries its ears semierect. The eyes are dark but may be any shade between black and brown, depending on the color of the coat; this also applies to the color of the nose. The coat is of medium length with abundant 'trousering' and tail feathering. In some areas of its home country its ears are cropped and the tail docked, but this is generally considered undesirable.

The color varies: white, black and white, fawn, pepper and salt, and tricolor are acceptable. In particolored dogs, a white collar is considered very desirable. The height at the shoulder is about 20 to 25 inches.

Anatolian Karabash Dog *Turkey*

The Karabash is an ancient breed – a powerful and tough dog closely related to the Mastiff – which for centuries has been used as a guard dog to protect sheep from marauding wolves. Outside Turkey it is almost unknown.

It is a big, heavy dog with a large head. Its eyes are golden brown and set well apart; its tail is long and curls into a ring with a suggestion of a flag.

The color varies from cream to fawn, but may also be brindle with a black mask and black ears. The weight is about 88 to 143 pounds; height at the shoulder is 26 to 30 inches.

Basset Griffon Vendéen *France*

This is another rare French breed. Despite its name, it has more in common with the Dachshund and Dandie Dinmont than a Basset. The Griffon Vendéen comes in two varieties: Grand and Petit. The main difference – apart from size – is that the smaller has a shorter foreface.

Both Grand and Petit, however, are rectangular in build and have a rounded skull and a marked stop. The eyes are large and dark; the ears are long and pendulous. The tail is long and thick and carried fairly high; the coat is profuse and coarse.

Both varieties may be self-colored, particolored, or tricolored in a variety of shades. The Grand is 15 to 17 inches at the shoulder, and the Petit is 13 to 15 inches.

Beauceron *France*

The Beauceron – sometimes called the Berger de Beauce or the Pastor de Beauce – is a French shepherd dog and one of the fairly rare breeds. It resembles the Dobermann Pinscher, being usually black and tan, red, gray, gray with black markings, or black. The Beauceron has a long, flat, wedge-shaped head with erect ears, usually cropped. The eyes are dark in black-haired dogs, otherwise they may match the color of the coat. The tail is long and carried

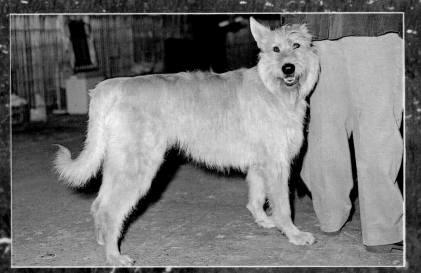

low; the coat is short and smooth. The height at the shoulder is 25 to 28 inches for dogs, 24 to 27 inches for bitches.

Berger Picard *France*

This is a French sheepdog from Picardy, which has much in common with its Belgian relatives, the Groenendael and the Tervueren. It is a powerful, muscular dog with an alert, intelligent expression. Its eyes are hazel brown and its ears are erect. Its tail curls into a slight ring at the end and, when the dog is in action, is carried in a delicate curve upward but not over the back. The shaggy coat is 2 to 3 inches long, and shorter on the head.

The color of the Berger Picard is usually gray with black, red, or blue shadings. The height at the shoulder is 24 to 26 inches for dogs and about 2 inches less for bitches.

Berger des Pyrénées *France*

The Berger des Pyrénées comes from the same area as the Pyrenean Mountain Dog. Both breeds were used as sheepdogs but, while the Pyrenean was often called upon to defend the flock against wild animals, the main task of the Berger des Pyrénées was to keep the sheep together. It is more closely related to the larger Briard and is generally just a smaller version.

According to the breed standard, the Berger des Pyrénées is 'full of nervous energy' and very active. The eyes are expressive and chestnut brown in color. The ears are profusely feathered giving the impression of being broader than they are high. The tail is bushy, set low, and curled into a ring at the end. The coat is fairly short, always very thick, and with a texture like a 'mixture of goatskin and fleece.'

The color varies considerably: different shades of gray with or without black (and white markings on head, feet, and chest), black with or without white, or even piebald. The height at the shoulder is 16 to 20 inches for dogs, proportionately smaller for bitches.

Bleu de Gascogne *France*

Three breeds of French origin use the name Bleu de Gascogne ('Blue Gascon'). The Grand Bleu de Gascogne, a Basset, is the smallest of the three (the height at the shoulder is between 12 and 15 inches); it is used to hunt hare. The second variety, the Petit Bleu de Gascogne, is a small, blue tracking dog, differing from the Grand Bleu only in size (19 to 22 inches at the shoulder). The third variety, the Bleu de Gascogne Petit Griffon, is wire-haired and similar in some ways to the more common Griffon types. It is extremely rare, has slightly smaller ears than its 'blue' relatives, and 17 to 21 inches tall at the shoulder.

Bracco Italiano *Italy*

There are two varieties of this pointing dog, the Piedmont Bianco Arrancio (orange and white) and the Lombardy Roano Marrone (chestnut roan).

The Bracco Italiano is well built with a flesh-colored nose and yellow eyes. Its ears are long and pendulous like a Bloodhound's, and its coat is short and shiny. Size varies from 22 to 25 inches at the shoulder.

Cesky Terrier *Czechoslovakia*

The Cesky Fousek is an extremely rare terrier and there are very few of the breed outside Czechoslovakia. In conformation the Cesky looks like something between a Kerry Blue Terrier and a Sealyham. It is a sturdy, stolid little dog with short legs, and it is said to have a pleasant temperament. The color is blue, gray or brown with

Far left, both: Berger Picard.
Below left: Bracco Italiano.
Below right: Grand Bleu de Gascon.

lighter markings on the head, neck, chest, and underside of the body. The height at the shoulder is 11 to 14 inches.

Drentse Patrijshond *Netherlands*
The Drentse Patrijshond is a pointing gundog and a water retriever; its temperament, adaptability, and intelligence also make it an excellent pet. It is little known, however, outside the Netherlands.

It resembles the German Long-haired Pointer, and has a very thick coat with long, wavy fringes on the ears and tail. The color is white with brown or orange patches. The average shoulder height is 24 inches.

Drever *Sweden*
The Swedish Drever, a tracking hound with an excellent nose and a good voice, looks like a slender Basset. Its origins are German and, until it was renamed in 1947, the breed was known as the Dachsbracke. Numerically it is one of the largest breeds in Sweden, but it is little known outside Scandinavia. (In Denmark it is bred under the name of Strellufsstövare.)

The Drever is a sturdily built dog with long ears. The basic color is white with reddish-fawn markings. The height at the shoulder for dogs is 12 to 16 inches.

Epagneul de Pont Audemère *France*
This spaniel breed, rare even in France, is supposedly descended from a cross between an old French spaniel and the Irish Water Spaniel. In general it resembles the latter.

The Epagneul de Pont Audemère has a brown nose, amber-colored eyes, and a thick, slightly wavy coat; the tail is usually docked. The color is chestnut, sometimes with gray markings. The height at the shoulder is 20 to 23 inches.

Gascon Saintongeois *France*
This hound is rare even in France and virtually unknown elsewhere. The two varieties, Grand and Petit, are identical, except for size and similar in type to the Grand Bleu de Gascogne.

The breed is short-haired and is distinguished by a long head with long, thin ears which hang in folds. The color is white with black markings. The height at the shoulder for the Grand is 25 to 28 inches for dogs, 24 to 26 inches for bitches; for the Petit, 23 to 25 inches for dogs, 21 to 23 inches for bitches.

German Hunt Terrier *Germany*
The Deutsche Jagdterrier is extremely rare. It is unrelated to the terriers of Britain and Ireland and more heavily built. Its head is flat and it is broader between the ears than the Fox Terrier, which it resembles. It has powerful jaws and its nose is usually black. The eyes are deep-set and, according to the German breed standard, 'dark with a determined expression.'

The coat is very thick, coarse, and rough and the color predominantly black, grayish-black, or dark brown. The height at the shoulder for a dog is about 16 inches, the weight is about 22 pounds.

Glen of Imaal Terrier *Ireland*
The Glen of Imaal Terrier was not officially recognized by the Irish Kennel Club until 1933, although the breed had been used for badger and otter hunting for centuries, primarily in County Wicklow where it is considered to have originated. As a dog bred to 'go to ground,' it is strong, courageous, and, above all, quiet; it is still a working dog rather than a pet.

The Glen of Imaal Terrier is a heavily built, powerful little dog with short, sturdy legs, slightly bowed in front. It has small dropped ears and brown, intelligent eyes. Its tail is docked and carried upward; its coat is fairly long and very coarse.

Accepted colors are bluish-gray with or without tan, and wheaten. The height at the shoulder is about 14 inches; bitches are invariably smaller.

Lundehund *Norway*
The Norwegian Lundehund is unique in that it has five fully developed toes on each foot; it takes its name from the 'lunde' bird (the puffin) which it used to hunt. It has lived for centuries mainly on the islands of Vaeroy and Röst, and the breed is rare even in Norway; outside Scandinavia it is hardly known at all.

The Lundehund is a lively little spitz. Its unusual feet have exceptionally large pads and each leg has double dewclaws (the dewclaws are found on the inner side of the forefeet, corresponding with the human thumb in position. To give a cleaner and tidier line to the leg they are often cut off newly born puppies). The coat is close, sleek, and profuse. The color is gray, black, or brown with white markings. The height at the shoulder is 14 to 15 inches for dogs, 13 to 14 inches for bitches. The weight is about 13 pounds.

Nova Scotia Duck Tolling Dog *USA*
This breed is said to be derived from the Chesapeake Bay Retriever, although it looks more like a Golden Retriever. It is a working dog, a retriever, but used primarily to create a disturbance at a lake in order to drive the ducks toward the shore close

Above : Nova Scotia Duck Tolling Dog.
Right : Glen of Imaal Terrier.

enough for the hunter to get a shot at them.

The color of the Nova Scotia Duck Tolling Dog is fox red. The height at the shoulder for dogs is about 21 inches; the weight is about 50 pounds.

Sinhala Hound *Sri Lanka*
The Sinhala Hound is a native of Sri Lanka (Ceylon), which often lives in a semiwild state, scavenging for its food. In size and shape it resembles the Basenji but, unlike the Basenji, it does bark. The color varies, but brown and dark brown brindle are the most common.

Tibetan Mastiff *Britain*
Despite its name, the Tibetan Mastiff is officially regarded as a British breed, but it is said to be still used in Central Asia as a guard dog. It is large and heavy, closely resembling the St Bernard. Its skull is broad and deep, the ears are small, and the eyes deeply set. The tail is carried curled over the back; the coat is thick and profuse. The color is either black and tan, golden, or pure black. The height at the shoulder is 25 to 27 inches for dogs, 22 to 24 inches for bitches.

Tosa *Japan*
The Tosa is the Japanese Fighting Dog. It is of comparatively recent origin, having been bred during the second half of the nineteenth century specifically for public dogfighting contests. To produce a tough and savage fighter, the Japanese imported mainly European breeds and crossed Bulldogs with Bull Terriers, St Bernards, and Great Danes to produce a breed which closely resembles the Mastiff, although it is somewhat smaller. Public dog fights are now officially prohibited in Japan, although illegal fights are still staged privately. However, the Tosa has found a new role as a guard dog and is said to be becoming popular as a pet.

The Tosa is a tall, imposing, and powerfully built dog. It has a large head with small, amber-colored eyes and small, dropped ears. The tail is set high and reaches the hock; the coat is short, smooth, and hard.

The color is reddish-brown, white with red patches, or reddish-brown with red markings. The height at the shoulder is at least 24 inches for dogs and at least 21 inches for bitches.